A Stitcher's Christmas Album

by Patti Lilik Bachelder

CHITRA PUBLICATIONS

Chitra Publications
2 Public Avenue
Montrose, Pennsylvania 18801

First printing: 1992

Library of Congress Cataloging-in-Publication Data.

Bachelder, Patti Lilik, 1951-
    A stitcher's Christmas album / by Patti Lilik Bachelder
        p.   cm.
    Includes bibliographical references.
    ISBN 0-9622565-3-6 : $9.95
    1. Needlework--Patterns. 2. Christmas decorations. I. Title.
TT753.B33 1992
745.594' 12--dc20   92-33334
                                                      CIP

Editor: Patti Lilik Bachelder
Design and Illustrations: Mark D. Wayman
Photographs: Stephen J. Appel Photography, Vestal, New York

Acknowledgements

My thanks goes to Amy Cantone and Elaine Rink, who spent many hours sewing and hand quilting for me. I also want to thank my friends in the Broome County Quilters' Guild, Mary Caro, Jill Neebe, Ann Bronsky and Lee Fink, who worked on samples and proofed patterns, and Mark, for being a pleasure to work with. Thank you all for the gift of friendship. Special thanks to our Art Elves, Pamela Moss Watts, and Angela A. Carpenter.

Dedication

This book is dedicated to Emily, who brags about me to her friends and shares her cat, Spitfire, with me; and to my ghosts of Christmas Past.

Introduction

I learned to sew when I was 13 years old. By the time I was 25, the serious stuff like men's shirts and pleated skirts gave way to dolls modeled after my friends and whimsies like dragons and bears who reveal their personalities as they come to life. But I have always had the most fun sewing for Santa. Everyone who knows me, knows that Christmas is "my" season. Used to be, I could tell you how many days were left on any given day of the year!

I love how friendly everyone is in December, in spite of how busy they are, and the shine on the world from the twinkle of lights on trees. I love bell choirs and carols played on acoustic guitars, and family traditions and holiday gatherings with friends. I love filling the house with the smells of holiday menus and cinnamon sticks simmering on a back burner. I especially enjoy how some people loosen the reins on their inner child, just for December; the man who wears a candy cane in his jacket pocket, the woman who ties a jingle bell around her wrist. I have lived in Florida, where poinsettias grow outdoors, and in New England, where I learned to make Snow Pudding. And I have spent all of my adult Christmas Eves wishing for snow on Christmas morning. I am like a child when my wish comes true, and then I make snow angels! My daughter Emily has outgrown them, but I don't think I ever will.

And oh, I do love presents, giving them more than getting them! I sew for Christmas almost year-round. Almost everyone gets something from my heart and hands, whether it's the gift itself or the box it comes in or a small token of friendship. The mailman picks up my handmade cards for delivery and expects to find homemade jellies and cherried cranberries in the mailbox on Christmas Eve. Some people have saved every card I've made, and just about everyone I know has at least one "Grimble" ornament on their tree. (For most of my life, I've called Christmas "Grimble." I borrowed the word from John Lennon's 1964 nonsensical book, *In His Own Write*. He used it in a "bah, humbug" way but I redefined it and use it as an adjective, a noun and a verb. We enjoy a Grimble feast, wrap Grimbles and go Grimbling, which could mean shopping or caroling or anything elfish. I even have a rubber stamp that says "Merry Grimble"!)

I can't resist making something small that's cute or quilted or just says "Christmas" (or "Grimble"!) and I had a lot of fun with the hodgepodge of designs in this book. Most take just an hour or two to make; the wallhangings take about a day to cut and piece. If you're pressed for time, like I usually am, spend a morning practicing machine quilting—you'll be pleasantly surprised at how easy it is to machine quilt these small pieces. And, like me, you'll be happy to see your finished projects begin to stack up.

No matter how large or small, Christmas gifts from your heart and hands are the best. May the spirit of Christmas reside with all of us year-round.

Merry Grimble!

CONTENTS

Some Tips and Hints About Sewing

Some of my points don't match or have been cut off a bit, but that's okay with me. When I first learned how to quilt, I would take things apart and re-sew them until every point was true. But I was so busy seeking perfection that I didn't finish many things. Several thoughts came together for me at one time and I became more productive. I wasn't quilting because I wanted to win contests, I was doing it for myself. And I liked the way my "imperfect" patchwork looked—it looked handmade, not manufactured. As long as I did my best, my work looked good. If I had to trim off a few points in order to make a block "square," that was okay, because the blocks would go together in straight rows and the overall effect of the finished work was wonderful. Those missing points were never missed! So just relax and have fun with the patterns in this book. It's okay if your work isn't "perfect."

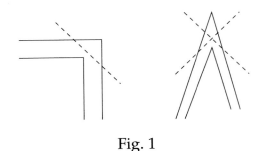

Fig. 1

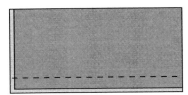

Fig. 2

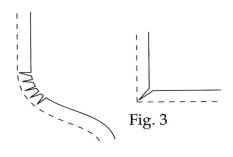

Fig. 3

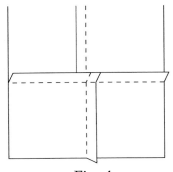

Fig. 4

In general

All of my ornaments were made from scraps, so sometimes there isn't much of a materials list. I've estimated fabric requirements in most cases; 1/8 yard (4 1/2" x 44") or a "fat quarter" (18" x 22") of each fabric will do for the ornaments. Keep a basket on your sewing table and toss in the scraps as you work. When you need "the perfect red" or "snow fabric," you'll enjoy looking through your holiday scrap basket! Use low-loft bonded batting or fleece for beards and "fur" trim, either sewn in like fabric or hand stitched on top.

This is not a "learn how to sew and quilt" book, but the directions with each pattern are fairly inclusive. Many of the designs were made using "no template" techniques; others can be sewn by hand or machine. To sew by machine, adjust the stitch length to 12-14 stitches/inch. For hand piecing, sew with a "between" (a sharp quilting needle). For hand appliqué, use a "sharp" (finer and sharper than a between). The higher the number, the shorter the needle and the smaller your stitches will be. My favorite needle is a #10 John James. Use good quality thread in a color that matches the fabric.

Sew 1/4" seam allowances; trim to 1/8" to reduce bulk wherever necessary. Trim seam allowances across corners at a 45° angle to reduce bulk. Trim points sharply. (Fig. 1) Grade seam allowances when a dark fabric might show through light fabric. (Fig. 2) Clip inside curves and angles for easier turning and a smooth look. (Fig. 3)

Press seams toward the darker fabric; do not press them open, as in garment construction. Press rows so intersecting seams will oppose each other, thereby laying flat. (Fig. 4)

Hand sewing

Cut your thread about 18" long. Longer thread will spin and knot or fray from the wear and tear of previous stitches. Thread the eye onto the beginning of the thread, not the end that you cut. During its manufacture, thread is twisted and going "with the grain" will make it easier to thread the needle. It might be easiest to thread the needle from the spool and then cut the thread.

Make a small, neat knot. Large knots will wear a small hole in the fabric, and it doesn't take long. Hold the needle and thread as shown. (Fig. 5) The fingers of the right hand should grab the end of the thread and the fingers of the left hand should wrap the thread around the needle three times. The right hand slides up and covers the wraps at the same time the left hand pulls the needle through. It's kind of like making a French knot without any fabric.

End off with a small, neat knot, too. Nancy Pearson, a master appliqué artist, taught me this nifty knot in one of her classes. (Fig. 6)

Appliqué with as "blind" a stitch as possible. Begin with the knot on the underside and pull the needle up through the background and the turned edge of the appliqué shape in one motion. Pierce the background in almost the same spot you came out of and glide the point about 1/16" away from the first stitch. Come up again through the background and the edge of the appliqué. Continue sewing in this manner, making closer stitches in points, inside angles and concave curves to prevent clipped threads from popping out. (Fig. 7)

Use a thimble! If you don't, the needle will literally drill into your fingertip. It's very painful. (I can't hem a pair of pants without a thimble now!)

Change needles whenever they bend or become blunt.

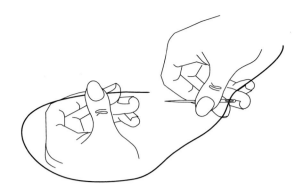

Fig. 5

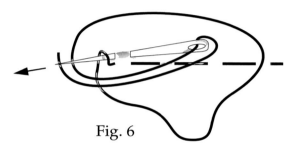

Fig. 6

Writing on fabric

The easiest way is to do the writing or drawing before sewing. Cut a piece of freezer paper the same size as the fabric you wish to write on and iron the shiny side to the wrong side of the fabric. I've tried many different brands of permanent markers and prefer Pigma 01; I use the larger 05 for some drawings. Practice on scraps to develop a light touch so the ink will glide onto the fibers rather than spread into them. Press for several minutes to heat-set.

To write on a straight line, lightly mark a few lines on the fabric with a hard pencil and a ruler, or make a good copy of your work and trace on a light box. I use the "Give Me Light!" light box; it's portable and affordable (see resources.)

Draw each word slowly but steadily. Make round areas and descenders full. (The descender is the part of a letter, usually lower case, that falls below the line, as in p, g, j.) Keep the angles and openings consistent so the letters will relate to each other. Go over lines to darken and strengthen them. For a calligraphic look, thicken the lines on just the right or left sides. Don't fill a space completely; a few skipped areas will look more realistic. With practice, your everyday handwriting can look like John Hancock's!

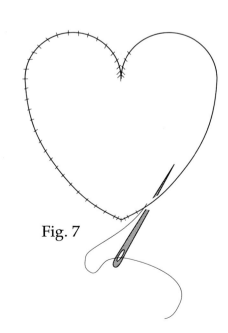

Fig. 7

Making and using templates

Cut templates (and fabrics) as you need them. Use clear plastic and do not include the seam allowance in your templates. For multiple cuts with a large rotary cutter, layer up to

8 fabrics and press them to help the layers "stick together." Tape your template to the top layer of fabric, then line up your ruler to add 1/4" all around and cut all the pieces at once. Some patterns refer to "R". This means reverse the template when cutting fabric.

Sew first, cut later

Gift-Giving Santa's tiny mittens have nice curves because they were cut after sewing. The arm piece is cut out and a square, larger than the mitten template, is sewn to each "wrist." The template is traced on the square to match the wrist. Fronts and backs are pinned together and the entire piece is sewn *on the pencil line*. The mittens are trimmed to 1/8" and clipped, then the piece is turned right side out.

Layer and sew

I like small, flat fabric ornaments, so many of these are not stuffed. The front and back pieces are placed right sides together on top of a piece of low-loft batting and pinned all around. The three layers are seamed together at the same time, leaving an opening for turning. If you'd like to add some stuffing, add enough to "plumpen" without "stuffing."

"Leave an opening for turning"

The easiest way to do this and still have nice, sharp corners, is to sew three sides plus a bit in from each corner of the fourth side. The opening will be easier to sew closed, too. If it's not specified, choose a spot that's unobtrusive, like the bottom or a straight edge. Avoid curves and corners. (Fig. 8)

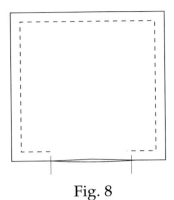

Fig. 8

Turning

Turning small pieces well is very important, and it isn't hard. Separate the two layers with your fingertips and place the eraser end of a pencil against one layer. Then feed the fabric over the eraser, enough so that you can wiggle the pencil through the tube to the opening. Grab the fabric that shows and carefully pull the rest through the opening, smoothing it as you go. Be sure to poke the corners out well, so they're square instead of rounded. An orange stick (from the manicure kit you received for Christmas several years ago) is handy for this. Do not pick at the points with a pin; the threads of the fabric will break, making a fuzzy point or even a hole.

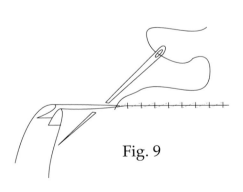

Fig. 9

Stitching the opening closed

Use a blindstitch and thread that is the same color as the piece you're sewing. (Fig. 9)

Marking and basting for quilting

My favorite marking tool for straight lines is drafting tape. It's not as sticky as masking tape, which will pull the fibers of the batting through the fabric and leave a heavy, unattractive "beard" on your project. For other marking, I use a Dixon chalk pencil (red on dark fabric) or Berol® Verifine® pencil (silver on light, yellow on dark fabric).

Baste the backing, batting and quilt top together with brass safety pins to keep the layers from shifting during quilting.

Quilting

Hand quilt with quilting thread. Begin by popping the knot through the top layer and burying it in the batting. (Fig. 10) Sew short, even stitches. Their length and distance apart should be about the same. Push the needle up and down, perpendicular to the surface. End with a small, neat knot a stitch length away from the last stitch; pop it below the surface and bury it in the batting. Bring the needle out about an inch away and clip. (Fig. 11)

For machine quilting, use nylon quilting thread on the top of the machine and thread to match the color of the backing in the bobbin. Use the "Big Foot" quilting foot or change to your machine's darning foot. Lower the feed dogs so you can move your project freely; this will also prevent pleating and puckering. Do not turn the fabric; instead, glide it evenly right or left, up or down. Sew slowly and move the piece with regularity to ensure even stitching. Sew around the pins or remove them as necessary.

Binding the edges

Use a rotary cutter and ruler to trim batting and backing even with the quilt top; measure the edges. Cut enough 2 1/2" strips of fabric on the straight grain and press lengthwise, right side out. Leaving the first 6" free, machine sew to the right side of the quilt, beginning at the center of the bottom edge. At the corners, stop stitching 1/4" from the edge and backstitch. Fold the binding up and away, then refold, matching the edges. (Fig. 12)

Leave 6" free at the end. Overlap both ends and pin-mark a match point for a seam. Trim (do not unpin), leaving 1/4" for seam allowance. Open binding, sew seam and refold binding. Finish sewing binding to quilt top. Fold the binding to the back of the quilt and blindstitch.

Sewing a hanging sleeve

Cut a length of fabric the width of your project by 7". Sew a 1/4" hem on the short ends. If the quilt has not been bound, fold the strip lengthwise and press. Pin the raw edge to the top edge of the quilt. Bind as usual, catching the sleeve in the binding seam. Blindstitch the fold to the quilt back to finish. For bound quilts, sew the long edges of the sleeve, right sides together, to form a tube. Turn and press. Blindstitch the top and bottom to the quilt back.

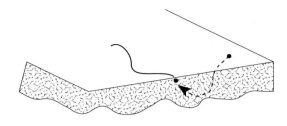

Fig. 10

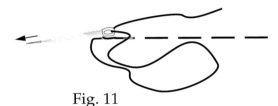

Fig. 11

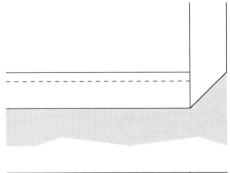

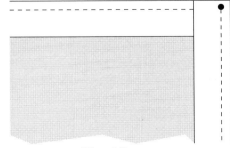

Fig. 12

Brittany's Stocking

The trick with stencilling is to load the brush with paint, then stamp most of it out before doing the actual painting. Your results will be soft and evenly colored, except where you want to add extra color for shading. Spruce up uneven edges and add details with Pigma pens.
Mark, who designed this book, became a father this year. I thought it would be fun to collaborate on a stocking for Brittany's first Christmas, so I used his design for this stocking.

Materials

1 yard ecru cotton
1 yard light-colored plaid for lining
(2) 18" x 24" pieces of batting
Crystal or pink Dizzle Dizzle paint
X-Acto® knife & new blade
No. 12 stencil brushes, one per color
Fabric or stencil paints
Black Pigma or IDenti-pen (or embroidery floss)

Templates on page 62 & 63

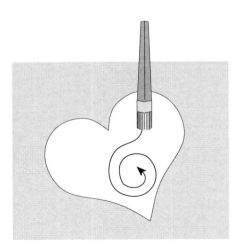

Fig. 1

Cutting the stencils

A stencil is required for each color. Check the craft stores for plastic film or waxed stencil paper. See what's available at the hardware store (7mm plastic?) and stationery store (overhead projection film?). If your film or paper is rolled, trace so that it curls downward. That will help keep the stencil close to the fabric.

Using a fine-point marker, trace the pattern for one color with solid lines, plus one or two shapes from another color with dotted lines. The dotted lines will be your registration marks, so use the same shapes on each stencil.

Cutting stencils takes longer than painting them. The best work surface is a piece of glass, because the point of the knife can't get stuck. The knife will glide through the plastic, allowing for smooth, continuous cuts. Try an old mirror, or tape the edges of an old piece of glass. If that's not an option, stack newspapers and cut stencils slowly so the knife won't snag. Move the plastic against the blade, if it's easier.

Cut out areas that will be painted. Cut curves with a continuous motion, beginning at the top and drawing the knife toward you; try not to stop until you reach an angle. Cut angles by inserting the knife point in the angle and drawing the knife downward. If you cut into an area that wasn't meant to be cut, just tape both sides to seal the cut line.

An individual hole punch is great for small circles. Obviously, the hole will be close to the edge of the paper or plastic; just tape another piece on so paint won't go off the edge.

Painting

Craft stores carry an astounding array of stencil paint colors; you can also use acrylics, and colors can be mixed. Heat setting makes them permanent. Most of my brushes are number 12; some don't have numbers on them. They're about 3/4" across, which I find adequate for large and small areas.

With a piece of shirt cardboard below it, tape the fabric to the work surface. (If it isn't taut, wrinkles will be painted in.) Tape the first stencil in place on the fabric. Squeeze just a bit of paint onto a folded paper towel, or use a popsicle stick to remove some from the bottle. A little goes a long way! Dip the brush into the paint and swirl it on the paper towel to remove most of it. The brush should look almost dry.

Be prepared to get some paint on your fingers, as you'll want to hold parts of the stencil down to be sure the brush won't go underneath them. Bounce or swirl the brush to paint, putting more pressure on areas that you want to look shaded and less on areas that will look like light is shining on them. Let dry according to directions on the paint bottle and press to set (Fig. 1).

Clean up

Before they dry, wash the brushes with soap and water, rinsing until the water is clear. Wrap a rubber band tightly around the bristles of each brush. Wipe the stencil clean with a damp sponge and roll it for storage. Better yet, share it with a friend!

To make the stocking

1. Trace stocking pattern; extend top by 3" to allow for cuff. Layer ecru cotton with plaid, wrong sides together, and cut out front; reverse pattern and cut out back.

2. Make these 5 stencils:

    1. Red: ribbon, pocket, hat. Cut out the centers of the bow and save them.

    2. Brown: mouse

    3. Red: ears, nose

    4. Green: heel

    5. White: eye

3. Paint each stencil. Using tape rolls, position the centers of the bow in place; they don't have to be exact. Hold them down as you paint around them.

4. Wipe the stencils clean and reverse them to paint the other side, if desired.

5. Using a light box or window, trace details with a black Pigma or IDenti-pen. Write the year, too. Practice writing the name and trace your best effort. If you want to go over it with machine quilting, move the piece slowly and deliberately for a machine embroidery effect. Rest your eyes if they grow tired. Or outline details and write the name in satin stitch embroidery.

6. Add some Dizzle Dizzle to make things sparkle. Squirt a bit on your fingertip and spread it around on the fabric. Let dry overnight.

7. Quilt stocking if desired. I pressed on a freezer paper heart and stitched around it.

8. Cut out and sew the extra ribbon pieces together, leaving the top open for turning. Trim corners and clip into the indentation. Turn and press. Pin on the stocking front (Fig. 2).

9. With right sides together, sew the lining to the front across the top. Repeat with the back pieces (Fig. 3).

10. Lay front and back pieces together and sew all the way around, leaving a 4" opening for turning in the lining (Fig. 4).

11. Clip curves, turn and machine stitch opening closed. Push lining down inside stocking and turn a 3" cuff to the outside. Sew a loop to the top and hang.

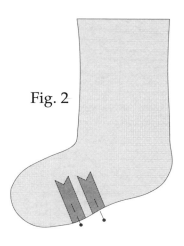

Fig. 2

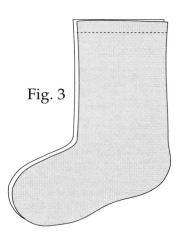

Fig. 3

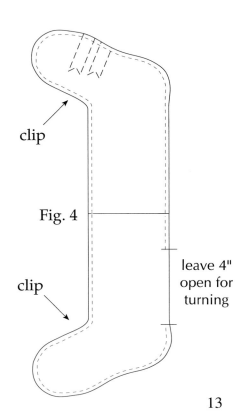

clip

Fig. 4

clip

leave 4" open for turning

13

Kids & Patches Stocking

Hooray for kids and Christmas! If you plan to make a lot of these boy or girl blocks at once, label the strips to keep them organized. Accurate measuring and cutting is essential. I used plaids and didn't worry about matching seams for a primitive stocking. Of course, you can match your seams if you want to! And you can make it with or without a patchwork cuff.

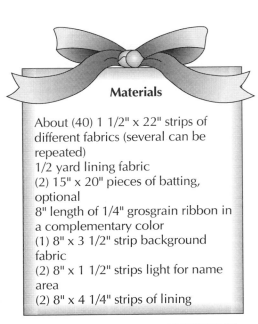

Materials

About (40) 1 1/2" x 22" strips of different fabrics (several can be repeated)
1/2 yard lining fabric
(2) 15" x 20" pieces of batting, optional
8" length of 1/4" grosgrain ribbon in a complementary color
(1) 8" x 3 1/2" strip background fabric
(2) 8" x 1 1/2" strips light for name area
(2) 8" x 4 1/4" strips of lining

Templates on page 62 & 63

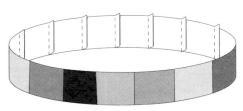

Fig. 1

The patchwork fabric

1. Sew the 40 strips together lengthwise. Press the seams in one direction.

2. Lay this strip set horizontally on your cutting mat and slice the entire piece into 1 1/2" segments. Check your cutting angle once or twice as you go and trim a bit to straighten the angle, if necessary.

3. Sew half of the strips into circles by joining the 1 1/2" sides (Fig. 1).

4. Lay an unstitched strip on the mat (Row 1) and lay a circular strip next to it (Row 2). Move the circle one square at a time until you have a "match" that you like, then remove the stitching where the strip will begin. Press seams so they oppose those of the first row, if necessary, and stitch the 2 rows together. Press.

5. Sew an unstitched strip to the second row, turning it so the order of the fabrics isn't identical to the first row.

6. "Match" another circular strip, remove the stitching, press it and sew it to the third row.

7. Add an unstitched strip, turned so the fabrics "match" Row 1.

8. Continue adding strips to create a scrappy patchwork fabric that measures about 21" x 30".

9. If desired, place the patchwork on a piece of batting and machine quilt it. (Brush the lint from the feed dogs and bobbin area afterward.)

10. Trace the pattern on page 62-63. Lay the pattern diagonally on the patchwork; align the top so it runs corner-to-corner through one row of patchwork squares. Pin along the outline; reverse the stocking pattern and make sure the patchwork is large enough for two pieces. (If it's not, realign the pattern angle so two pieces will fit.)

11. Cut the front. Cut two lining pieces on the straight grain and set them aside. Reverse the pattern and cut another patchwork stocking for the back.

Make the blocks for the cuff

Make a full-size drawing of the desired block(s) on graph paper. As each piece is cut, lay it in place on a sheet of paper, referring to your drawing. When the pieces are all laid out, take the sheet of paper to the sewing machine and sew each row together. Finger-press as you sew, rather than using the iron.

3" Girl Block

Background fabric
(1) 7/8" x 4 1/2" strip. Cut into
(3) 1 1/4" segments for Row 1.
(1) 1 1/8" x 4" strip. Cut into (2)
1 5/8" segments for Row 2.
(1) 3/4" x 3 1/2" strip. Cut into
(2) 1 1/2" segments for Row 3.
(1) Cut (1) each A and A/reversed for Row 4 from template.
(1) 1 1/4" x 4" strip. Cut (2)
1 1/2" segments and (1) 3/4"
segment for Row 5.

Hair fabric
(2) 7/8" squares for Row 1.

Flesh fabric
(1) 1 1/4" x 1 1/8" (face)
(1) 7/8" x 4" strip. Cut (4) 1" segments for hands and legs.

Dress fabric
(1) 7/8" x 2" strip. Cut (2) 1" segments for sleeves.
(1) 1 1/8" x 1 1/2" strip for bodice.
(1) 1 1/8" x 3" strip. Cut (1) B
from template..

Shoes fabric
(2) 7/8" x 3/4" strips

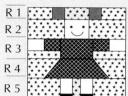

1. Sew pieces into rows and join the rows together as you go.
   Row 1: background/hair/background/hair/background. Press seams to the left.
   Row 2: background/flesh(face)/background. Press seams to the right. Sew Row 2 to Row 1 for upper half of block.
   Row 3: Sew one arm: flesh(hand)/sleeve. Sew the other arm: sleeve/flesh(hand). Press seams toward sleeve. Sew hand/sleeve to background strip. Press toward background. Sew to either side of dress bodice strip. Press toward dress bodice.
   Row 4: Sew background to either side of skirt and press seams away from skirt. Sew Row 3 to Row 4.
   Row 5: Sew flesh (leg) to shoe. Press seam toward black. Sew the background strip in between and press toward shoes. Sew a background strip to either side of this unit and press seams toward segments.
2. Sew Row 5 to Rows 3 and 4 for lower half of block.
3. Sew upper half to lower half. Press seams as they fall. Be careful not to distort the seam lines as you press, so things won't look crooked.
4. Trim block to square it up.

3" Boy Block

Background fabric
(1) 3 1/2" x 7/8" for Row 1.
(1) 1 1/8" x 3 1/4" strip.
Cut into (2) 1 1/8" x 1 5/8"
segments for Row 2.
(1) 2 1/8" x 3" strip. Cut
into (2) 2 1/8" x 1 1/2"
segments for Rows 3 and 4.
(1) 3/4" x 1 1/4" strip for
between legs.

Flesh fabric
(1) 1 1/4" x 1 1/8" rectangle for face.
(2) 7/8" x 2" strips. Cut into
(4) 7/8" x 1" segments for
hands and legs.

Shirt fabric
(1) 1 1/2" x 1 1/8" rectangle.
(2) 7/8" x 1" strips for sleeves.

Shorts fabric
(1) 1 1/2" x 1 1/8" rectangle.

Shoes fabric
(2) 7/8" x 3/4" strips.
Small scrap for hair.

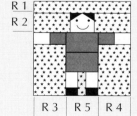

1. Sew pieces into rows and join rows as you go.
   Row 1: Background strip.
   Row 2: Sew scraps of hair to upper edges of face, at an angle. Lay hair right side down on face. Sew and flip back. Press. Following the shape of the face piece, trim the excess hair to match the rectangle. Repeat for the other side of the hair. Sew background/face/background for Row 2. Sew Row 2 to Row 1.
   Row 3 and 4 (left and right sides): Sew the first arm: flesh/sleeve; sew the other arm: sleeve/flesh. Press toward sleeves. Sew to background, referring to diagram. Press toward background. Set aside.
   Row 5: Sew shirt to shorts. Press toward shorts. Sew legs to feet. Press toward feet. Sew background strip between legs and press toward feet. Sew background pieces to either side of this unit and press toward background. Sew Rows 3, 4 and 5 together for lower half of block.
2. Sew upper half to lower half. Press seams as they fall. Be careful not to distort the seam lines as you press, so things won't look crooked.
3. Trim block to square it up.

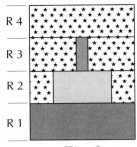

R 4
R 3
R 2
R 1

Fig. 2

To make 2 package blocks:

1. Cut 2 strips 1 1/4" x 2 3/4" from patchwork fabric for Row 1.

2. Cut (4) 1" x 1 1/4" rectangles from same background as the 3" block. Cut 2 rectangles 1 3/4" x 1 1/4" from package fabric and sew background rectangles to either side on the 1 1/4" sides for Row 2. Press seams in one direction (Fig. 2).

3. Cut (4) 1 1/4" squares from background. Cut (2) 1 1/4" squares from a patchwork fabric and sew background squares to either side for Row 3. Press seams in one direction.

4. Cut 2 strips from background, 1 1/4" x 2 3/4" for Row 4.

5. Press seams in one direction.

6. Sew package blocks to either side of the 3" boy or girl block to make the cuff unit.

Finishing

1. Write the child's name on the light strip, leaving about 1/2" of space above and below the name. If you goof, just cut another strip and try again. Sew the name strip across the bottom of cuff unit. Sew the other light strip across the bottom of the 8" x 3 1/2" background strip. The light portion is the bottom of the unit.

2. Sew the top of the cuff unit to the top of the lining piece you cut for the front of the stocking, right sides together. Press seams toward stocking.

3. Sew the top of the background/light unit to the top of the lining piece you cut for the back of the stocking. Press seams toward lining.

4. Sew an 8" x 4 1/2" lining piece to the top of the patchwork stocking front, right sides together. Repeat with back. Press toward lining.

5. Sew the top of the front lining to the top of the front patchwork (Fig. 3). Fold wrong sides together and press a crease across the top. Repeat for the back.

6. Open out both pieces. Right sides together, sew all around, leaving an opening in the lining near the "ankle" for turning. (Begin just above the ankle and stop when there is about 4" left.) If you didn't quilt the patchwork, stitch this seam twice for added strength; the edges of the patchwork are all on the bias and one row of stitching could easily pop with use.

7. Turn and sew the opening closed. Push the lining down inside the stocking and fold the cuff down.

8. Sew the ribbon inside the stocking for a hanging loop.

9. Fill with goodies on Christmas Eve!

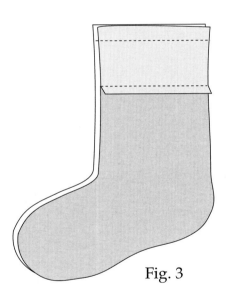

Fig. 3

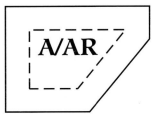

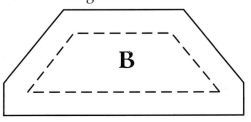

Angel Chorus

Angels flutter by themselves or wing-to-wing as an Angel Chorus garland. Make a dozen in a jiffy!

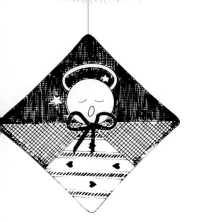

1. Cut A triangles. Fold the gold fabric lengthwise into fourths and cut a 2 3/8" wide strip. Cut the strip into 2 3/8" squares. Cut the squares in half diagonally, corner to corner (Fig. 1).

2. Cut B squares. Fold dress fabric the same way and cut a 2" strip. Cut the strip into 2" squares. If you use a stripe, cut bias strips and then cut squares, so the stripe will go downward instead of at an angle (Fig. 2).

3. Cut C triangles. Fold the blue fabric the same way and cut a 3 7/8" strip. Cut the strip into 3 7/8" squares, then cut the squares in half corner to corner.

4. Sew an A triangle to one side of the B square. (If using a stripe, be sure the square is turned so the stripe lines up with the sewn edge.) Chain-sew all of these units at the same time. Cut apart and finger-press the seam allowance toward A (Fig. 3).

5. Chain-sew A triangles to the other side of the A/B units. Cut apart and use an iron to press the seam allowance to A (Fig. 4).

6. Chain-sew A/B/A units to C triangles. Press the seam toward A/B/A (Fig. 5).

7. Use a square ruler to trim the blocks square, if necessary. (Mine always need trimming; I don't press "square"!)

8. Apply Wonder Under® to the muslin. Cut out 12 circles using a large thread spool as a pattern and press one to the blue side of each block, just above the intersection of the three bottom pieces. (Or appliqué each face in place.)

9. Paint or embroider a halo around each face. Draw eyes with a brown or black Pigma 01 pen.

10. Pin each block face down on the strip of backing fabric. Cut apart but do not unpin. Lay the sandwiches on a piece of batting and pin through the batting. Cut apart and stack the pinned sandwiches next to your sewing machine.

11. Sew all four sides, leaving an opening in the center of one side for turning.

12. Clip corners and turn. Blindstitch opening closed.

13. Blindstitch 4" pieces of ribbon to the sides of 11 blocks and tie the blocks together for the garland. Stitch a ribbon hanger on the last block and hang it on the tree.

Materials
for a dozen angel blocks

1/8 yard each:
Gold or yellow for wings
Print or stripe for dress
Blue stars print for sky
Backing fabric
Scrap of muslin for faces
Pellon Wonder Under®
Glittering Gold Scribble Paint
(The last two items are not necessary if you plan to appliqué the face and embroider the halo.)

Fig. 1

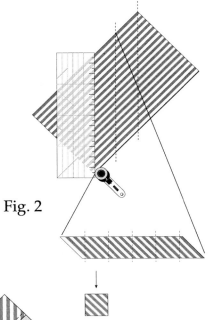

Fig. 2

Fig. 3

Fig. 4

Fig. 5

17

Baby's First Christmas

A little egg in a pink or blue diaper marks baby's first visit from Santa!

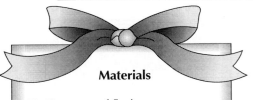

Materials

(1) 6" square of flesh
(1) 6" square pink or blue (diaper)
5" piece of 1/2" ruffled eyelet lace
6" length of pink or blue ribbon
Small gold safety pin
Embroidery floss for eyes and mouth

Templates on page 61

Fig. 1

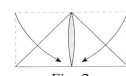

Fig. 2

1. Fold the flesh fabric in half. Trace egg pattern on top layer and cut out both layers at once.

2. Draw or embroider eyes and mouth. Write or embroider "Baby's First Christmas (year)" on the back piece, above the diaper line.

3. On front, pin eyelet lace around top of egg. Pin ribbon loop at top and stitch lace in place. Trim excess (Fig. 1).

4. Cut diaper square in half; (2) 3" x 6" pieces. Fold lengthwise and press, wrong sides together. Keep folded and cut in half; (4) 3" x 1 1/2" pieces.

5. With the fold at the top, pin a folded rectangle on the bottom of the egg front. Pin another one on the bottom of the egg back. Trim to the shape of the egg.

6. Fold another rectangle (Fig. 2):

7. Center this piece on the diaper front, with the folds on the inside. Trim to shape.

8. Place front and back right sides together and sew, using the lace seam as a guide. Leave 2" open for turning.

9. Turn and pin diaper with safety pin. Stuff gently and blindstitch the opening closed.

Friendship's Offering

Offer your hand with a floral motif or a small heart. Beautiful on a Victorian tree or as a package trim for someone special. Call it "cute" if you use cotton fabrics and a candy cane motif!

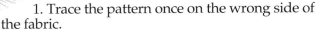

1. Trace the pattern once on the wrong side of the fabric.

2. Use a light box to determine placement and fuse a flower or other printed motif to the palm of the hand (right side). Or position a small heart and hand appliqué in place.

3. Fold the square right sides together into a rectangle, with the tracing on top. Lay very thin piece of batting below it and pin together.

4. Machine sew with a *very* close stitch length (about 16 stitches/inch), being careful to follow the pencil line exactly so the fingertips will be well defined. Leave the wrist open for turning. Trim, leaving a scant 1/8" seam allowance. Clip into angles as close to the seam as you can. I did not use it, but you may want to finish satin seams with liquid seam binding. When I turned my first version right-side out, some of the woven threads popped through because I clipped too deeply; my second one was perfect.

5. Hand quilt to define fingers.

6. Fold a 3" length of lace (or batting or fur for the cute version) around the wrist, turning the raw edges under, and blindstitch.

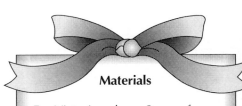

Materials

For Victorian glove: Scrap of satin and a small floral motif; 3" scrap of 1/2" lace
For "Cute" glove (not shown): Scrap of cotton and a small Christmas motif; 3" scrap of 1/2" batting or fur
Scrap of Wonder Under®
Liquid seam binding (optional)

Templates on page 61

Roly Poly
Santa Angel

He's a round and jolly old elf with heart-shaped wings. And he's easy to make from a strip set.

1. Make 2 matching 4-row strip sets: red/flesh/red/black (as listed). Press all seams toward black.

2. Trace the Santa pattern on the wrong side of one strip set, matching the guidelines with the seams.

3. With the traced fabric on top, place the two strip sets right sides together and pin so that seams match. Place a piece of batting below them and pin.

4. Machine stitch on the pencil line, all the way around. (Do not leave an opening for turning.) Trim to 1/8" seam allowance.

5. Using the pattern as a guide, mark a 2" line in the center of the "trim placement" area on one side of the ornament. Separate the two layers of fabric and cut a slit. Turn right side out through the slit. Do this carefully, so the slit doesn't tear. Poke out all the edges, smoothing the curves.

6. Imagine that Santa has arms and place a mitten at the end of one arm. Position it so that it's aimed outward and partially covers part of his body. It should "touch" the trim placement guideline. Place a mitten on the other side of the same arm and match them. Hand-stitch the two mittens together and tack to the body as needed. Repeat for the other arm.

7. Starting at the edge of an arm, tack the long strip of batting in place around the front and back of the ornament (and over the slit), using the placement line as a guide. Trim any excess and tack the edges together.

8. Sew the short strip of batting around the bottom of the hat.

9. Using white floss, sew a blanket stitch around the edge of the beard and tack it in place.

10. With red floss, sew a blanket stitch around the edge of the wing piece. Sew to the back of the ornament with 3 or 4 cross-stitches or other decorative stitches.

11. Quilt a line of running stitches to define the arms and legs.

12. Roll a ball of batting and glue it to the top of the hat (or use a white pompom). Sew a red thread through the hat for a hanger.

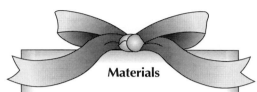

Materials

(2) 2" x 6" red print
(2) 1 1/2" x 6" flesh
(2) 2 7/8" x 6" red print
(2) 1 1/2" x 6" black
(1) 7" x 1/2" batting (waist trim)
(1) 2 1/2" x 1/2" batting (hat trim)
(1) wing, batting (do not add seam allowance)
(1) beard, batting
(4) mittens, white felt (do not add seam allowance)
Red and white floss
White pompom (optional)

Templates on page 64

Baby Stocking

Flip-and-sew strips directly onto the batting for a quick, quilt-as-you-go stocking. Fill it with candy canes and hang it on a doorknob or the Christmas tree. Or make the cuff from fabric instead of fleece and write the dog's name on it—Santa just might fill it with doggie treats!

Materials

About (15) 12" x 1" strips of various darks and mediums
(2) 12" x 1 1/2" strips for toe and heel
About 18" of piping
12" square of batting
12" square of lining
6 1/2" x 2" strip of fleece or bonded batting

Templates on page 61

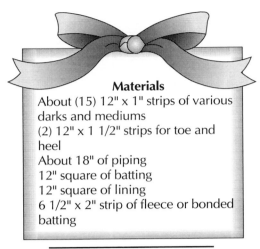

Fig. 1

Fig. 2

Fig. 3

Fig. 4

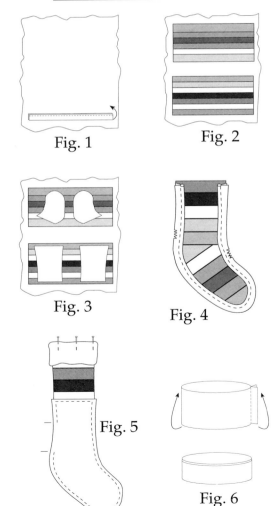

Fig. 5

Fig. 6

1. Lay the first 1" strip right side up on the bottom of the batting. Place another 1" strip on top of it, right sides together, and sew a 1/4" seam. (Fig. 1)

2. Open out and finger-press. Lay a 1" strip on top of the second strip, right sides together. Stitch, open and finger-press. Continue adding 1" strips until the work measures 6".

3. Lay the toe strip right side up on the top of the batting. Sew (4) 1" strips in place and end with the heel strip. (Fig. 2)

4. Cut a top and bottom piece, then reverse the patterns and cut another set. (Fig. 3)

5. Sew the top and bottom patchwork pieces together.

6. Pin piping along the edge of one piece of patchwork. Change to the zipper foot and sew in place. You may want to clip the piping along the toe and heel. (Fig. 4)

7. Pin and sew the front and back patchwork pieces together, using the piping seam as a guide. Turn right side out.

8. Tape the top and bottom patterns together and cut two lining pieces. Sew them together, leaving the area between the dots open for turning. Do not turn.

9. Sew the ends of the fleece cuff together and turn right side out. Slide it over the top of the stocking and pin in place, lining up the seam with the back seam of the stocking.

10. Tuck the patchwork stocking inside the lining (the raw edges will be on the outside) and re-pin the stocking/fleece/lining together at the top edge. (Fig. 5)

11. Stitch all around the top edge of the stocking. Wiggle the lining until the patchwork stocking can be pulled through the opening and turn right side out. Stitch the opening closed. Push your fingers into the toe of the lining piece and work the lining to the inside. Adjust the cuff.

12. Sew a hanging loop in place.

For a fabric cuff instead of a fleece cuff, cut a 6 1/2" x 4" rectangle from a light-colored fabric. Sew the short ends together. Bring the raw edges together and press (the seams will be inside). Pin the raw edges to the raw edges of the stocking and continue with Steps 9 through 12. (Fig. 6)

Folk Stars

They're free spirited! Make a bunch to string together for a garland or just a pair to drape over a branch or doorknob. Or make gift tags—dark stars with light centers that say "To" and "From." These are great for popping into Christmas cards, too.

1. Trace patterns on wrong side of fabric, 2 of each star for each ornament. Cut out, leaving 1/4" seam allowance on large stars and 1/8" seam allowance on small stars.

2. Appliqué small stars in center of large stars.

3. Pin front and back right sides together and stitch all around, leaving an opening for turning.

4. Cut a 12" length of sisal and knot each end. Blindstitch one knot to a star point. Sew the other knot to a second star.

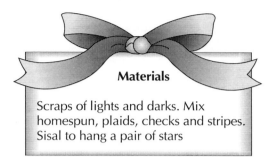

Materials

Scraps of lights and darks. Mix homespun, plaids, checks and stripes. Sisal to hang a pair of stars

Templates on page 61

Merry Kitty

Use fabrics that will depict your cat's colors. If yours is a black cat, jazz it up by sewing seed beads around the edges of each piece so it will sparkle on the tree.

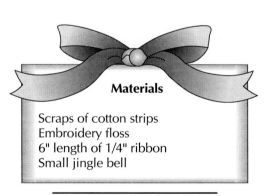

Materials

Scraps of cotton strips
Embroidery floss
6" length of 1/4" ribbon
Small jingle bell

Templates on page 61

1. Make templates that include the seam allowance.

2. Make a crazy patch: Lay a small strip right-side up in the center of a 6" piece of batting. Place another strip right-side down and sew the two strips together. Open and finger press. Continue adding strips, changing the angles every time to give the cat some character. Finally, sew a large black scrap right-side down over 1/3 of the patchwork, at a 45° angle.

3. Place a 6" square of backing fabric behind the patchwork, wrong sides together. Place the templates on the patchwork so a good "face" area will show. Cut both layers at once, leaving 1/4" seam allowances.

4. Place face pieces right sides together and sew around, leaving an opening for turning. Repeat with ears. Trim seams to 1/8", turn right-side out and blindstitch opening closed.

5. Embroider features. Use 6 strands of floss for whiskers, leaving 1/2" free and securing with a backstitch; knot in back to end off.

6. Work a blanket stitch by hand around the three pieces. (See page 24.)

7. Position ears behind face and blindstitch in place.

8. Sew a small bow and a jingle bell at the cat's neck. Thread a 6" length of monofilament through the top and knot for a hanger.

Gift-Giving Santa

Pipe cleaners make his arms bendable. Wrap them around a heart or spread them wide to hold something special, like a "Welcome" sign!

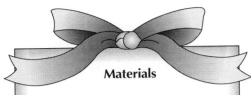

Materials

Fat quarters or scraps: flesh color, white Aida or cotton, dark red, bright red small plaid, small check.
Long pipe cleaner

(1) A flesh (face)
(1) B and BR white Aida cloth or cotton (beard)
(1) C white Aida cloth or cotton (back of head)
(2) dark red hearts
(2) 8 1/2" x 1 1/4" strips plaid (arms)
(1) 7/8" x 3/8" strip bonded batting (fur)
(1) 1 1/2" x 6" strip check (hat)
(4) 2" squares red (mittens)

Templates on page 64

Fig. 1

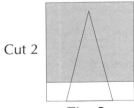

Cut 2

Fig. 2

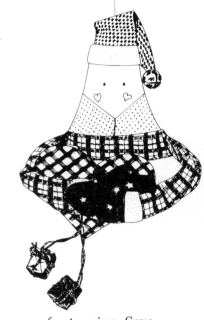

1. Face: Embroider or draw eyes. Sew B to A. Do not stitch into the seam allowance where B and BR will meet. Sew BR to A. Stitch B and BR, being careful not to stitch into A (Fig. 1).

2. Hat: Sew batting to short ends of 1 1/2" x 6" strip. Align template D over seam and trace (Fig. 2). Cut 2 and sew one to top of face and one to head piece C.

3. Arms: Sew batting to short ends of the plaid strips. Trim to same width as arms. Sew red squares to the batting. Trace mitten E on the red squares on either side of one arm piece; do not cut (Fig. 3).

4. Pin front and back together, matching seams. Stitch all the way around, leaving the bottom open for turning. Sew slowly around the mittens so they will stay "round." Clip and trim where necessary (Fig. 4). Turn right side out.

5. Stuff Santa's hat halfway up. Stuff his face firmly. Using paper scissors, cut the pipe cleaner to 10" and insert it into the arms. Sew opening closed.

6. Sew the heart. Clip point to 1/8". Turn through opening and stuff lightly. Bend Santa's arms to hold it. Tack his hands in place.

7. Fold the hat forward and sew a short length of thread through the fold for a hanger.

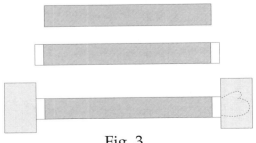

Fig. 3

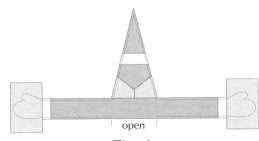

open

Fig. 4

Gingerman

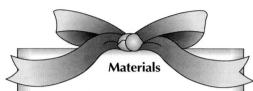

I once lived in a wooded area and made my own pine garlands by cutting boughs and wiring them together. They were great draped around the front door, but indoors, I learned the hard way—cover the mantel with a piece of worthless fabric before laying the pine boughs on it, to catch the pitch drippings! Now I drape my house with artificial pine boughs that are spruced up with patchwork. Many ornament patterns would make cute garlands. Make a string of gingermen to drape in a doorway!

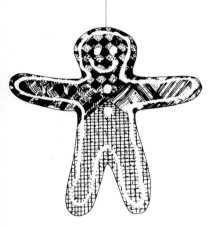

1. Sew 7 Four-Patch blocks using pleasing combinations of 3 1/2" squares (Fig. 1).

2. Trace the gingerman pattern on the wrong side of each block, aligning the cross mark with the intersection of the four patches. (I made one man with the pattern lined up straight, just for fun.)

3. Pin each block right side down on a square of backing fabric and sew the outline of the man, leaving an opening for turning.

4. Clip angles and trim seam to 1/8". Turn and stuff.

5. Blindstitch the opening closed.

6. Sew six men together, hand to hand, for a garland.

7. Outline each man with paint, about 1/4" from the edge. Don't forget to "dot his eyes"!

8. Sew a hanging loop on the last man and hang him on the tree.

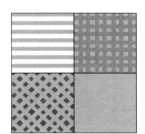

Materials

Materials for 7 men (6 to hold hands and 1 for the tree!)
14 light or medium 3 1/2" squares
14 dark 3 1/2" squares
(14) 6" squares of backing fabric
White Scribble Paint for frosting

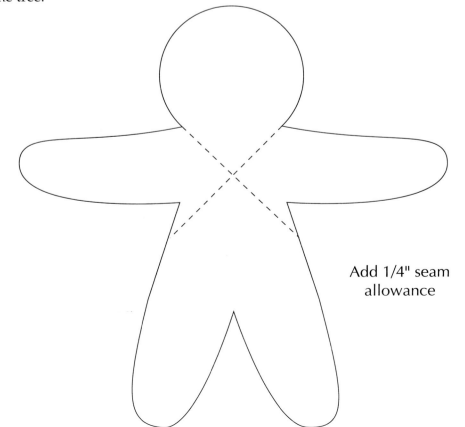

Fig. 1

Add 1/4" seam allowance

Moon-Faced Santa

He's so easy to make, you'll have this Santa hanging on the tree before he nods off! Two strips of fabric and a combination template make this sleeping Santa a real quickie.

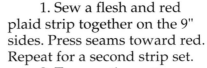

Materials

for 2 ornaments:
2 strips flesh, 4" x 9"
2 strips red plaid, 3" x 9"
Scraps of thin bonded batting
2 small jingle bells
Scrap of pink felt for cheeks
White pearl cotton

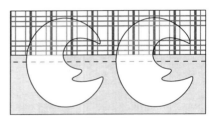

Fig. 1

1. Sew a flesh and red plaid strip together on the 9" sides. Press seams toward red. Repeat for a second strip set.

2. Trace entire pattern on template plastic, marking placement line for seam. Trace template twice on wrong side of one strip set, 1/2" apart (to allow for 1/4" seams) (Fig 1).

3. Place the 2 strips sets right sides together, with the tracing on top, and pin on a strip of thin batting.

4. Machine stitch on the pencil lines, leaving an opening for turning. Trim seams to 1/8" and clip curves.

5. Turn each Santa and fold the open edge to the inside. Pin closed.

6. From batting, cut 2 strips 5/8" x 3 1/2" for hat trim and 4 beards.

7. From pink felt, cut 4 cheeks.

8. Pin beard pieces in place and blanket stitch all around. Begin at the back of the head and stitch through both sides until you reach the nose. Do not end off. Position a felt cheek piece under the batting and continue to blanket stitch through the front and cheek only, finishing at the top of the head. Stitch a short row of blanket stitches on the other side of the face, beginning at the nose (Fig. 2).

9. Wrap a 5/8" x 3 1/2" strip of batting around the bottom of the hat and blanket stitch to the back of the hat.

10. Embroider the eyes or mark with a black Pigma 01 pen.

11. Sew a jingle bell to the end of the hat.

12. Sew a 10" length of thread as indicated on the pattern and knot for a hanger.

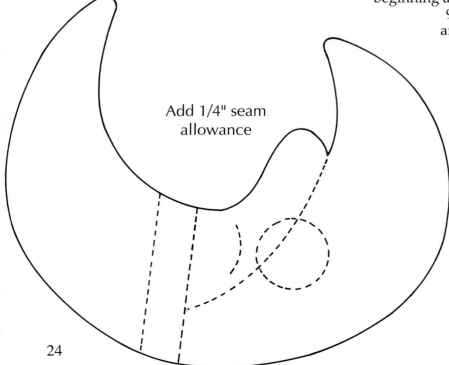

Add 1/4" seam allowance

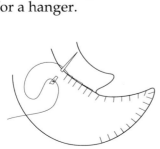

Fig. 2

Amish Quilts

Make them in brilliant solids with black for bold contrast like real Amish quilts or use prints for a homespun look. "Press" with your finger, not an iron.

Amish Bars

1. Sew the red and white strips together alternately, lengthwise. Press seams in one direction. Trim edges to "square up."

2. With top edges even, sew the purple strip to one side. Trim excess. Sew remaining strip to the other side and trim. Press toward purple. Repeat for top and bottom. "Square up," if necessary.

3. Sew and trim the black strip the same way: side/side/top/bottom. Press toward black.

4. Place quilt top and backing right sides together and place on the batting. Sew all around, leaving an opening for turning. Trim corners and turn. Sew opening closed.

5. Tack a thread to top corners and knot for a hanger.

Diamond-in-a-Square

1. Sew a short green strip to top and bottom of red square. Press toward green.

2. Sew a purple square to each end of 2 short green strips. Press toward green.

3. Sew strips from Step 2 to opposite sides of red square unit, matching seams.

4. Sew triangles to top and bottom. Finger-press toward red. Sew triangles to sides. Press toward red. Trim edges to "square up," if necessary.

5. With top edges even, sew the white strip to one side of the quilt top. Trim excess. Press toward white. Sew remaining strip to the other side and trim. Repeat for top and bottom.

6. Apply the long green strip the same way, pressing toward green.

7. Finish as in Steps 4 and 5, Amish Bars.

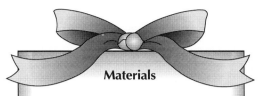

Materials

Amish Bars
(4) 3/4" x 2 1/4" strips red
(3) 3/4" x 2 1/4" strips white
(1) 3/4" x 12" strip purple
(1) 1" x 14" strip black
(1) 4" square each, backing and batting

Diamond-in-a-Square
(1) 1 1/2" red square
(2) 2" red squares cut once on the diagonal (4 triangles)
(4) 3/4" x 1 1/2" strips green
(1) 1" x 18" green
(4) 3/4" squares purple
(1) 1" x 16" white
(1) 5" square each, background and batting

Roman Stripes
(2) 3/4" x 16" strips for striped portion of 5 blocks
(2) 3/4" x 8" strips for striped portion of 4 blocks
(1) 2" x 15" contrasting fabric
(2) different 20" x 3/4" strips for borders
(1) 8" length of sisal for hanger
5" square of batting

Roman Stripes

1. After each sewing step, trim seams to 1/8". Sew the 3/4" x 16" strips together lengthwise. With edges even, sew (1) 3/4" x 8" strip to one side; do not lift presser foot. Slip the other 3/4" x 8" strip in place and continue sewing. Press seams in one direction (Fig. 1).

2. Sew the strip set to the 2" x 15" strip. Sew a seam on both long sides of the strip, but do not turn the tube right-side out. Trim left edge "square."

3. Using a square ruler and rotary cutter, cut 9 triangles. Align the 45° diagonal on the edge of the strip and cut (Fig. 2).

Re-align the 45° diagonal to cut the other side of the triangle (Fig. 3).

Re-align the ruler and cut 7 more triangles. Be sure that your cuts make pointed, rather than blunted, triangles. Open the blocks and press seams in same direction.

4. Arrange blocks into rows of 3 across and 3 down and sew into horizontal rows. Press seams for Rows 1 and 3 in one direction; press seams for Row 2 in opposite direction. Sew rows together to form quilt top. Press seams as they fall.

5. Sew the 2 border strips together lengthwise. Miter borders (see Hints and Tips About Sewing).

6. Finish as in Steps 4 and 5, Amish Bars.

7. Knot either end of the sisal and blindstitch the knots to the top corners.

Fig. 1

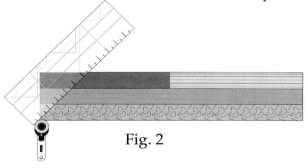

Fig. 2

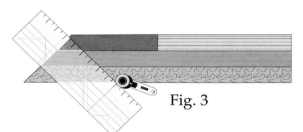

Fig. 3

Crazy-Patched Hearts

For me, satins and lace are like expensive chocolates: I indulge only once in awhile and savor the riches. Add these fancy hearts to your collection of Victorian ornaments, or hang them on a doorknob to say "Welcome, friend" year-round.

1. The irregular patchwork fabric is created the same way as for Merry Kitty. Add lace by placing it on top of a fabric scrap and sewing the two pieces to the foundation fabric as one. Or sew lace over seams after the fabric scraps have been sewn on. Cover the 4 foundation squares with piecing.

2. Trace the heart pattern on the wrong side of 2 patchwork squares. Place a square of batting behind the other 2 squares. Pin the traced squares on top of the batted squares and machine sew each one on the pencil line, leaving an opening for turning. Clip curves and the deep angle at the top of the heart.

3. Turn and stuff. Sew opening closed.

4. Sew one end of the 2' ribbon to the top of one heart. Sew the other end to the other heart. Make small ribbon bows and stitch or glue to the top of the heart. Add embellishments, if desired.

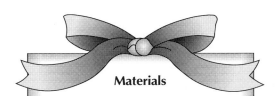

Materials

Scraps of fancy fabrics and lace
Scraps of decorative ribbons for bows
(4) 6" squares of muslin for foundations
(2) 6" squares of batting
2' length of 1/4" ribbon for hanger
Optional embellishments: buttons, charms, ribbon roses

Add 1/4" seam allowance

Santa Dolls, Big and Small

When I made the Santa ornament, I knew I had to make one that was big enough to hug!

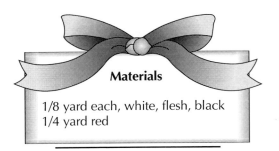

Materials

1/8 yard each, white, flesh, black
1/4 yard red

Templates on page 65

To make half a dozen ornaments
Cut these strips for the front of the dolls:
Hat/Trim/Face:
1 3/4" x 30" red for hat
3/4" x 30" white for trim
1 3/8" x 15" flesh for face
Mittens/Trim/Shirt:
(2) 1 1/8" x 30" black for mittens
(3) 3/4" x 30" white for trim
(2) 1 5/8" x 30" red for shirt
Pants/Trim/Boots:
1 3/4" x 30" red for pants
(2) 3/4" x 30" white for trim
1 1/4" x 30" black for boots
Beard:
(2) bias strips 3/4" x 2" white
Cut these strips for the back of the dolls:
Hat/Trim/Back of Head:
1 1/2" x 30" red for hat
3/4" x 30" white for trim
1 5/8" x 15" white for back of head
Mittens/Trim/Shirt back:
(2) 1" x 30" black for mittens
(2) 3/4" x 30" white for trim
(1) 3 1/4" x 30" red for shirt
Pants/Trim/Boots back:
Same as for front

Fig. 1

Ornament

Front

1. Sew hat/trim/face strips together. Press seams toward hat (Fig. 1).

2. Sew mitten/trim/shirt strips together for left and right side. Sew a trim strip between them. Press seams toward mittens (Fig. 2). Cut into 1 1/2" slices.

3. Sew boots/trim/pants/ trim strips together. Press seams toward boots (Fig. 3).

4. Sew shirt slices to flesh side of head strip set. Press seam toward shirt (Fig. 4).

5. Sew pants strip set to the other side of the shirt segments. Press toward pants (Fig. 5).

Back

1. Sew hat/trim/back of head strips together. Press toward hat.

2. Sew a trim strip and mitten strip to either side of the shirt strip. Press seams toward mittens (Fig. 6). Cut into 1 1/4" slices.

3. Make strip set for pants same as for front.

4. Sew head strip to shirt strip. *Do not add pants strip.*

Finishing

1. Trace pattern on front strip, matching lines for strip placement.

2. Press under 1/4" seam allowance of white edge on back pants strip. Press under 1/4" of the shirt edge on the other back strip.

3. Pin back head/shirt strip to front strip, matching seams and middle slices. Pin back pants strip in place, butting the 2 pressed-under seam allowances at the back waist.

4. Sew all around on the pencil lines. Cut dolls apart and trim to 1/8" seam allowance. Clip curves and turn through the opening in the back.

5. Stuff softly.

6. Holding the 2 beard pieces together, make 1/2" cuts every 1/8" for fringe. Keeping the pieces together as one, use a running stitch to sew them to the face, curving them as you sew.

7. Add dots for eyes with a Pigma pen.

19" Doll

1. Sew hat/trim/face strips together. Press seams toward hat.

2. Sew hat/trim/back of head (white) strips together. Press seams toward hat.

3. Sew mitten/trim/front shirt pieces together for left and right sides. Sew the red jacket pieces to either side of the 1 1/2" x 3 3/8" white strip. Press seams toward mittens.

4. Sew a white trim strip and black mitten strip to either side of the red "back of the shirt" strip. Press seams toward mittens.

5. Sew a waist trim strip to the bottom of the front and back shirt units.

6. Sew the front head unit to the top of the front shirt unit. Sew the back head unit to the back shirt unit.

7. Sew boot/leg strips together. Sew to front and back. Press seams toward boots.

8. Embroider eyes.

9. Lay front and back pieces right sides together and place on 2 pieces of batting. Pin the pattern in place, matching seams, and cut all four pieces at once.

10. Remove the bottom layer of batting and place it on top of the sandwich. Pin all 4 layers together. (The batting will help smooth out the stuffing.)

11. Sew together, leaving a 4" opening for turning in one leg.

12. Clip into angles and curves. Trim curves to 1/8" so they will turn smoothly.

13. Turn right side out. Stuff hat and head firmly, then stuff arms, legs and tummy firmly enough so Santa will stand up but soft enough to still be huggable. Blindstitch the opening closed.

14. Fold the beard strip in half lengthwise and press. Cut every 1/4", stopping 1/4" from the fold.

15. Sew the beard to the face by hand, using a long needle and three strands of white embroidery floss. Stretch as needed to make it curve.

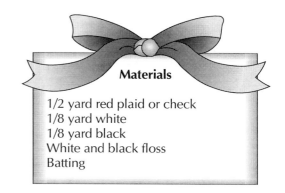

Materials

1/2 yard red plaid or check
1/8 yard white
1/8 yard black
White and black floss
Batting

Cut these pieces. (Mark each one as you cut.)
Red:
(2) 4 3/8" x 17" (hat)
(2) 3 1/2" x 4 1/2" (jacket front)
(1) 3 1/2" x 17" (jacket back)
(2) 4 1/4" x 17" (pants)
White:
(1) 3 3/8" x 17" (back of head)
(2) 1 1/2" x 17" (hat trim)
(4) 1 1/2" x 3 1/2" (sleeve trim)
(1) 1 1/2" x 3 1/2" (jacket center)
(2) 1 1/2" x 17" (jacket waist)
(2) 1 1/2" x 17" (pants trim)
Flesh:
(1) 3 3/8" x 17" (face)
Black:
(4) 3 1/2" x 3 1/4" (mittens)
(2) 2 3/8" x 17" (boots)

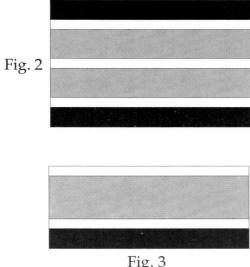

Fig. 2

Fig. 3

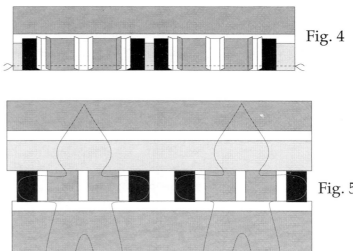

Fig. 4

Fig. 5

The Star of The Show

Make two: one to keep and one to give away! Or make a dozen and string them together for a garland. He's big enough to display on top of the tree.

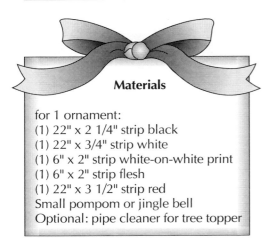

Materials

for 1 ornament:
(1) 22" x 2 1/4" strip black
(1) 22" x 3/4" strip white
(1) 6" x 2" strip white-on-white print
(1) 6" x 2" strip flesh
(1) 22" x 3 1/2" strip red
Small pompom or jingle bell
Optional: pipe cleaner for tree topper

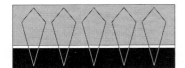

Fig. 1

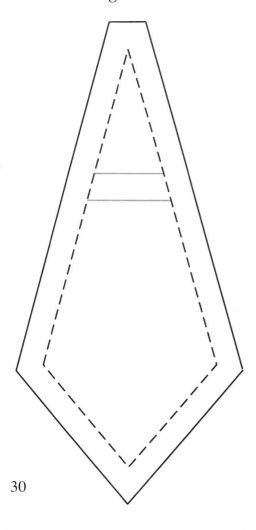

1. Sew long strips together: black, white, red. Reinforce the seams on the white and black sections with a second row of stitching. Press toward the black (Fig. 1).

2. Cut out 8 diamonds, placing the black/trim guidelines on the strip set.

3. Gently pull the black strip off the remaining strip set. Sew the flesh and white beard strips in its place.

4. Cut out 2 diamonds with the long point on the red, placing the black/trim guidelines on the red/white strips.

5. Draw the face.

6. Make 2 units using 4 arm/leg diamonds and 1 face/hat diamond each. *Begin and end each line of stitching 1/4" from the raw edge.* First, sew 3 diamonds together. Then sew 2 diamonds together. Align these pieces for one short seam; pin where they will meet in the center, pushing seam allowances out of the way. Sew and end off. Match the other seam, pinning at center, but this time, let the 2 seam allowances oppose each other. Pin the bottom seam down, out of the way. Pin the top seam up; it will be sewn over. (This will prevent a hole in the center if your seams don't match up perfectly.) Sew the last seam, *starting 1/4" from the outer edge* and ending exactly at the center. Do not sew across the seam lines.

7. Press the center seams in the direction of the last seam, fanning around the center.

8. Repeat with the remaining pieces. Carefully press the 2 stars flat. Trim points to about 1/8" seam allowance.

9. Pin stars right sides together, matching heads. Sew all around, leaving an opening in one leg for turning. Clip almost to the stitchline at each inside angle.

10. Turn and stuff smoothly. Leave the open leg unstuffed.

11. Fold the seam allowances in and pin the opening closed. Using black thread, blindstitch the boot and knot. Change to white thread, blindstitch the boot trim and knot, but don't cut the thread. Stuff the boot, leg and tummy. Pin and finish blindstitching.

12. Sew a pompom or jingle bell to the top of Santa's hat and sew a loop of thread through the hat for a hanger. Or bend pipe cleaner to find the center and secure the center to the middle of Santa's back. Bend around the top of the tree to hold him in place.

Vertical rows of background and candlestick fabrics make Candle Glow quick and easy to piece. The holly leaves can be hand appliquéd or fused in place. Page 43. And a special present—or a special friend!—deserves a special Gift Box. Page 55.

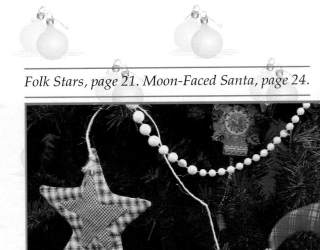

Gingerman, page 23. Baby Stocking, page 20.

Gift-Giving Santa, page 22. Angel, page 17.

Friendship's Offering, page 18. Roly Poly
Santa Angel, page 19.

Roman Stripes Amish Quilt, page 25. Angel Chorus garland, page 17. Star of the Show, page 30.

Baby's First Christmas, page 18. Amish Bars Quilt, page 25.

Small Santa Doll, page 28.

Merry Kitty, page 21. Diamond-in-a-Square Amish Quilt, page 25.

Holiday memories can be stored in a Photo Album designed just for the occasion. Page 50. The Diamond Tree wallhanging is a quick and easy one-patch project. Stitch shiny beads at intersections or tack garlands of "pearls" here and there. Page 44.

A row of four-patch Gingerman dolls make a garland of "cookies" so realistic, you'll want a bite! You could add a convincing holiday scent by tying cinnamon sticks between their hands. Page 23.

Flip-and-sew with fancy scraps and laces for a pair of Crazy-Patched Hearts to greet visitors year-round. Page 27.

A quartet of holiday pillows made with templates and quick-cutting techniques. Big Rudy, 14". Christmas Courtyard, 13". Cranberry Wreath, 15". Sprigs of Holly, 14". Page 39.

The recipients of Wonder-of-a-Kind Christmas cards will appreciate your sentiment over and over as these little wallhangings are unpacked each year. Page 53. So will the child who is given a Santa Doll to hug. Page 29.

Brittany's Stocking is an easy one-piece pattern. Stencil a holiday mouse in the "pocket" and embroider a special child's name by hand or machine. Page 12. Kids and Patches can be made for a girl or boy. This stocking is cut from strip-pieced fabric. Page 14.

The four blocks in Clara and Company are made from one basic design. A small change here and there make each character unique. Page 47.

Fill the pockets of Countdown to Christmas with tiny mementoes and hang one on the tree each day. Page 45.

Christmas Pillows

My sofa pillows change personalities with the seasons. I have a set of basic forms and Christmas pillows become sentimental Valentines when I change the pillow covers. Here are four blocks for Christmas, but you can make a pillow out of any block.

To make a block "pillow size," add borders or background, then measure the finished patchwork. It can be any shape: round, square, heart-shaped. Very small pillows need only be stuffed and stitched closed. Larger pillows can be stuffed and stitched, too, but if you want to "re-cover" them for the seasons, you'll need to make a pillow form and finish your blocks with an "envelope" closure.

To make a pillow form, add 1/2" to the measurements of your finished pillow top and cut two pieces of sturdy muslin this size. Sew around three sides and to the left and right of top center. Sew a second seam next to the first one for added strength.

Clip corners diagonally and turn. Use polyester stuffing to fill firmly; don't overstuff. Use good quality stuffing because it has a "memory." It keeps its shape, doesn't bunch up or separate and the finished piece will actually weigh less, too. After stuffing, blindstitch the opening closed.

When your pillow top has been quilted or embellished, add backing pieces to make an envelope closure for your pillow cover. The left and right sides of the backing should overlap each other by about 2" to create the opening. (Fig. 1)

To find the width of the backing pieces, measure halfway across the pillow top and add about 4" (more, if it's a very large pillow). This "facing" will give the opening some body. Cut two pieces this width by the height of the pillow top. Lay them right sides together with the pillow top.

Finger-press the center raw edges for a 1/4" hem, and sew. Lay the pieces in place and fold the center edges back about 2"; the 2 pieces should overlap by about 1 1/2". Press the folds. Pin the backing pieces in place and sew two rows of stitching around all 4 sides. Clip diagonally across the corners and trim excess batting and backing. Turn through the opening, poke out the corners and insert the pillow form.

Edge Treatments

You can add piping or ruffles to your block before sewing the backing pieces on. To make matching piping, purchase raw welting or filler cord (usually found in mail order sewing supply catalogs) or roping (found on the trim shelves in sewing stores). I usually use a 1/4" filler. Cut 1" bias strips and

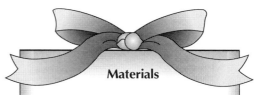

Materials

Each of these pillows requires about 1/2 yard of main fabric and 1/8 yard of accent fabric(s). Decide fabric placement using the block diagrams. Finish each pillow as instructed above.

Big Rudy
Requires tree print for background, 1 or 2 brown prints for antlers and face, and scrap of red for nose

Christmas Courtyard
Requires light solid for background of courtyard steps, dark or medium print for steps, 4 green prints and 4 green solids for trees and scrap of brown for trunks.

Cranberry Wreath
Requires 1 each light, dark-medium and medium green prints, dark red print and light background.

Sprigs of Holly
Requires 4 dark to medium green prints, a small scrap of red and 4 light to medium-light prints for backgrounds.

Fig. 1

seam them together to make one long length; you will need about 50" for a 12" block. Adjust the sewing machine needle so it is on the left side of your zipper foot. Lay filler on the wrong side of the bias strip and cover it, with the raw edges even. Sew down the entire length, with the foot against the filler.

To sew the piping to the block, begin at the bottom center of the block. Align raw edges of piping with those of the block and bring the end of the piping down into the seam allowance. Pin to first corner. Exactly at the corner, clip piping almost to the seam and bring it around the corner. Pin to the next corner and repeat around. Overlap piping at end, bringing the end into the seam allowance. Sew all around.

Lace is sewn on the same way. At the corner, ease in at least 1/4" (more for wider lace) so the ruffle will fan around the corner nicely when the pillow is turned right-side out.

Folded triangles, like the edging on Big Rudy, are made by folding a square in half and pressing, then folding the corners to the center and pressing. (Fig. 2)

They are pinned face down to the edge pillow top, raw edges even, leaving 1/4" seam allowance at the beginning and end of the row. Adjust placement as necessary so they are evenly spaced.

Pin backing pieces in place and sew from the other side, sewing over the seam made when the edge treatment was sewn in place.

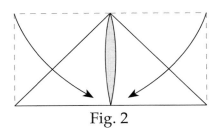

Fig. 2

Mark each set of pieces (A, B, etc.) as you cut.
Cutting
(32) 1 1/2" squares dark-medium green (A)
(16) 1 1/2" squares medium green (B)
(20) 1 1/2" squares red (C)
(16) 1 1/2" squares background (D)
(4) 2 1/2" x 1 1/2" strips background (E)
(8) 2 1/2" squares light green (F)
(4) 3 1/2" x 1 1/2" strips dark-medium green (G)
(2) 3 1/2" x 2 1/2" strips background (H)
(1) 3 1/2" x 7 1/2" strip background (I)
(4) 2" x 16" strips background (J)

Blocks for Christmas Pillows
Cranberry Wreath, 13" block

1. Arrange and sew A through F pieces to form 4 corner units. (There will be squares left over.) Sew together. Press seams symmetrically. (Fig. 3)

2. Arrange and sew A, B, C and G pieces to form 2 connector units. Press seams symmetrically. (Fig. 4)

3. Sew Rows 1 and 3: 2 corner units with a connector unit in between (each). Press seams in same direction. (Fig. 5)

4. Arrange and sew A, B, C, G and I pieces to form Row 2. Press seams opposite Rows 1 and 3. (Fig. 6)

5. Sew rows together.

6. Sew a border strip to either side; trim excess. Press away from block. Sew the remaining strips to top and bottom; trim and press.

Fig. 3

Fig. 4

Fig. 5

Fig. 6

Big Rudy, 14" block

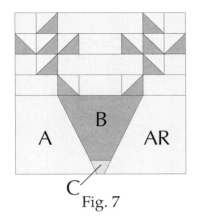

Fig. 7

1. Make antler units. Cut all the 2 3/8" squares diagonally in half once for 12 triangles each, brown and background. Chain-sew the long sides of the triangles together to make pieced squares. Cut apart and press seams toward brown.

2. Lay pieces in order and sew to form block. Press rows downward. (Fig. 7)

3. Add border strips to top and bottom; trim excess. Add border strips to side. Press seams away from block.

Cutting
(6) 2 3/8" brown squares for antlers
(24) 3 1/2" brown squares for edging
(1) A, main fabric (background)
(1) A/reversed, main fabric
(1) B, brown
(1) C, red
(4) 15" x 1 1/2" main fabric strips for borders
(6) 2 3/8" main fabric squares
(4) 2" main fabric squares
(2) 2" x 6 1/2" main fabric strips
(4) 2" x 3 1/2" main fabric strip

Templates on page 60

Christmas Courtyard, 10" block

Cutting
(4) 3 1/4" squares, dark or medium print (steps)
(1) 1 7/8" square, dark or medium (center)
(3) 1 7/8" squares, each green print, total 12 (tree tops)
(3) 1 7/8" squares, each green solid, total 12 (tree tops)
(1) 1 1/2" square, each green solid, total 4 (corners)
(18) 1 7/8" squares, background
(4) A, background
(4) AR, background
(4) B, brown
(1) C, each green solid, total 4

Templates on page 60

1. Make "pathway" units. Cut the 4 dark/medium squares in half diagonally both ways (16 triangles). Cut the 18 background squares in half diagonally once (36 triangles); set aside 4 of these. Sew the remaining 32 smaller background triangles to either side of the large dark/medium triangles. Chain-sew all the pieces to one side; cut apart and press toward background. Chain-sew the pieces to the other side; press toward background. (Fig. 8)

Sew 4 units together. Repeat three more times. Press seams upward. (Fig. 9)

2. Make center by sewing the 4 smaller background triangles you set aside to the remaining dark/medium square.

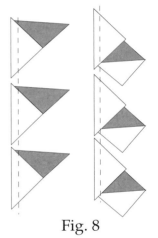

Fig. 8

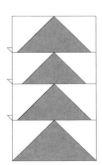

Fig. 9

3. Sew A and AR to B (do not stitch into seam allowances). Set-in C carefully by sewing A/C seam and backstitching; do not end off. Fold as necessary and sew C/B seam. Backstitch and sew C/A seam. Press seams toward A and C. Sew this unit to D triangle. Press seam toward A/B/C.

4. Cut all 1 7/8" squares for tree tops in half diagonally once for 24 triangles each, print and solid. Chain-sew together into pairs. Cut apart and press seams toward prints.

5. Arrange matching pieced squares, 1 1/2" corner square and D-trunk unit for each tree. Sew pieced squares into rows of 3. Press seams toward prints. Sew one row to D triangle. Sew a corner square to the other row and add to complete upper tree units. Press seams toward D. Repeat for all tree units.

6. Arrange 4 tree units and 4 steps units around the center unit. Sew units into 3 rows and sew rows together to form block. Press seams toward tree units.

Sprigs of Holly, 15" block

1. Using the same greens and the same backgrounds, sew green A's to background A's to form squares. Press seams toward green. Repeat A/A for all fabrics.

2. Arrange A/A units with B and C squares and sew into rows. Sew rows together to form units. (Fig. 10)

3. Sew D triangles together in pairs for 2 units. Press seams in opposite directions and sew together to form a square. Press. (Fig. 11)

4. Lay out sewn units with corner squares E (mix so backgrounds don't match). Sew into rows. Press top and bottom rows so seams are toward corners. Press middle row so seams are toward center. Sew rows together to form the block. Press seams in one direction.

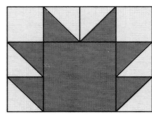

Fig. 10

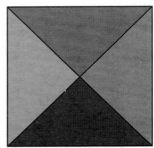

Fig. 11

Candle Glow

Great as a wallhanging in the dining room or a pillow in the living room.

1. Strips are cut 1 1/2" x 44", then small pieces are cut from strips. Mark each piece as you cut.

2. Cut 2 strips of striped fabric for candles and subcut into the following pieces. Cut (2) 6 3/4" lengths for the shortest candle rows 1 and 7. Cut (2) 8 1/2" lengths for candle rows 2 and 6. Cut (2) 10 1/2" lengths for candle rows 3 and 5. Cut (1) 12 1/2" length for the center candle row 4.

3. Cut 7 strips of background and subcut. Cut (8) 15 3/4" lengths for rows between candles. Cut (2) 9 1/4" lengths for the shortest candle rows 1 and 7. Cut (2) 7 1/2" lengths for candle rows 2 and 6. Cut (2) 5 1/2" lengths for candle rows 3 and 5. Cut (1) 3 1/2" length for the center candle row 4.

4. Lay pieces in order on work table. Sew background and striped pieces together for candle rows 1 through 7.

5. Sew rows together, alternating background and candle rows. Press seams in one direction. Trim edges "square," if necessary. The piece should measure approximately 15 1/2" square.

6. Sew the brown rectangle across the bottom. Trim, if necessary. Press seam toward brown.

7. Appliqué holly leaves and candle flames in place.

8. Sew border in place, mitering corners.

9. Prepare the quilt sandwich. Mark a quilting line diagonally, corner to corner. Repeat for other corners. Mark lines every 3/4" on either side of these lines. Quilt and embellish.

10. Sew a hanging sleeve to the back.

Materials

For a 21" x 24" wallhanging
3/8 yard diagonal stripe for candles
1 yard background and backing
Scraps of different greens
Border stripe; amount will vary, depending on the width of the stripe you choose
2 1/2" x 15 1/2" rectangle of brown for table
26" x 23" piece of batting

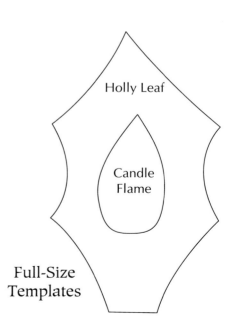

Holly Leaf

Candle Flame

Full-Size Templates

Diamond Tree

Say "welcome" by displaying this little wallhanging on the door.

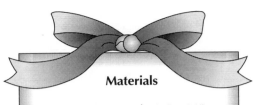

Materials

For an approximately 19" x 21" wallhanging
1/2 yard green
(20, total) 4 1/2" x 3" pieces of purples, reds, yellows
Scrap gold lamé for star
9" x 3" scrap of brown for trunk
2/3 yard backing
24" square of batting
Foamcore, approximately 18" square
2" of hook-and-loop closure tape
Small ring for hanger

Templates on page 64

1. Cut 25 green diamonds and 20 scrap diamonds.

2. The first (diagonal, right) row is made up of 5 green and 4 scrap diamonds. Sew alternately, beginning and ending with green. Press seam allowances to the left.

3. Sew remaining rows as follows, beginning at top:
Row 2: 4 each scrap and green, beginning with scrap. Press seams to the right.
Row 3: 4 green, 3 scrap, beginning with green. Press to the left.
Row 4: 3 each, beginning with scrap. Press to the right.
Row 5: 3 green, 2 scrap, beginning with green. Press to the left.
Row 6: 2 each, beginning with scrap. Press to the right.
Row 7: 1 each green, scrap, green. Press to the left.
Row 8: 1 each scrap, green. Press to the right.

4. Lay rows in order. Add a green diamond for Row 9 and sew rows together, butting seam allowances. Press seams toward bottom of tree.

5. With right sides together, place backing on tree and trim. Lay batting on top and pin all around. Sew around, from the patchwork side, leaving an opening on one side for turning. At the bottom, sew down the first diamond, then pivot by leaving the needle down and turning your work to sew the upward seam. Be sure to stitch up to the existing seamline, pivot and sew downward. Repeat to finish.

6. Along the bottom, clip into the angles. Turn right side out. Whipstitch the opening closed.

7. Quilt and embellish as desired.

8. Fold the brown rectangle right sides together, lay a piece of batting below it and sew the two long sides. Trim excess batting, turn and stitch opening closed. Center trunk and blindstitch to the back of the tree.

9. Place star fabric and lining right sides together. Trace star shape and stitch on the pencil line all around, leaving an opening for turning. Turn and blindstitch opening closed. Sew to top of tree.

10. Sew a ring on the back at the top of the tree to hang.

Countdown to Christmas

Fill 25 pockets with family mementoes and decorate an advent tree, one day at a time.

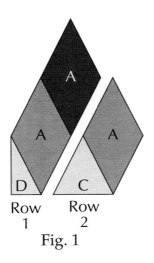

1. Fold red B diamonds in half, point to point, right side out, and press. Pin a folded B to the right side of a dark green A diamond. The red is slightly larger than the green, to make a roomy pocket. Pin 25 A/B diamond sets and machine baste each one. Remove pins.

2. Referring to the photo on page 38, sew A/B diamonds to medium green A diamonds to form diagonal rows from left to right. All C pieces are background. Begin with D background for Row 1.

Row 2: 1 C, 1 green A.
Row 3: A/B, A, C.
Row 4: 2 A, 1 A/B, 1 C. Begin with A, end with C.
Row 5: 2 each A and A/B, 1 C. Begin with A/B, end with C.
Row 6: 3 A, 2 A/B, 1 C. Begin with A, end with brown C.
Row 7: 3 A, 3 A/B, 1 C. Begin with A/B, end with C.
Row 8: 4 A, 3 A/B, 1 C. Begin with A, end with C.
Row 9: 4 A, 4 A/B, 1 C. Begin with A/B, end with C.
Row 10: 5 A, 4 A/B, 1 C. Begin with A, end with C.
Row 11: 5 A/B, 5 green, 1 DR. Begin with A/B, end with DR.
   (Fig. 1)
   Press seams in one direction, alternating each row.
   3. Sew rows to make tree.
   4. Sew bottom row of tree section: 10" background strip, background D/rev, 3 brown C, background D and 10" back-

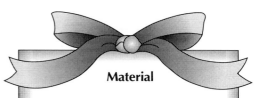

Material

1/2 yard medium green for tree
1/4 yard dark green for pockets
1/2 yard red print for pockets and binding
2 yards for background and backing
5" scraps of medium and dark reds and greens for border
6" square of brown for trunk
25 shank buttons

Templates on page 57

Cutting
25 A, dark green
30 A, medium green
20 A, red and green scraps
25 B, red print
8 C, background
4 C, brown
(2) 13" x 23" rectangles, background. Place right sides together and pin. Using a straight edge, draw a line from upper right corner to lower left corner. Cut 1/4" to right of the line for upper background triangles. Cut other background pieces from the excess.
14 D, background
14 D/rev, background
28 E, background
(2) 2 3/4" x 10 1/2" strips, background
(2) 3" x 7 1/2" strips, background
(4) 3" squares, background

Row 1   Row 2

Fig. 1

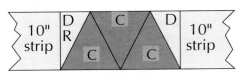

Fig. 2

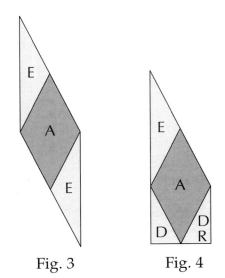

Fig. 3   Fig. 4

ground strip. Press seams toward brown. Sew across bottom of tree. (Fig. 2)

5. Sew upper background triangles to either side of the tree unit.

6. Side borders. Make 8 diagonal 3-piece units (4 per side). Press seams (4 in one direction, 4 in the opposite direction). (Fig. 3)

Make (4) 4-piece units (2 per side). Press seams (2 in one direction, 2 in opposite direction). (Fig. 4)

Arrange and sew into (2) 6-diamond rows, beginning and ending with a 4-piece unit. Sew to either side of the tree unit.

7. Top and bottom borders. Sew 4 units: (Fig. 5)

Sew a 3" square to one end of all 4 units. With 3" square in corner positions, sew a 7 1/2" background strip between 2 units. Repeat. Press. Sew to top and bottom of tree unit. Press.

8. Cut batting and backing 1" larger than quilt top and baste the layers together. Quilt as desired.

9. Trim edges and bind. Add a hanging sleeve.

10. Sew buttons to points of pockets. Hang mementoes from buttons.

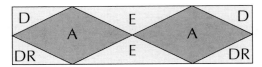

Fig. 5

Clara and Company

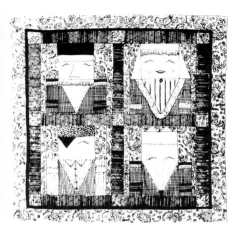

If you haven't seen a live performance of The Nutcracker, maybe this is the year to do so! Make this wallhanging as a memento of the occasion, for your own special ballerina or just for fun. One basic block pattern is used for Clara, the Mouse King, Herr Drosselmeyer and a Nutcracker Santa. Some of the pieces are cut every 1/4" for fringe and hair.

The Nutcracker Block

Requires only 2 templates: A and B
Also requires a stencil for the cheeks

1. Lay all pieces in order before sewing.
2. Unit 1: Head. Sew hat, brim and face together. Press seams toward hat. Sew short background strips to either side. Press toward background(Fig. 1).
3. Unit 2: Uniform. Sew A's to either side of B. Press toward A. Lay the mustache strip right side up on this unit and baste across the top (Fig. 2)

Sew both sleeves at the same time: Lay a yellow fringe strip right side up on top of the 2 1/2" x 3 1/2" sleeve strip and pin. Lay a black epaulet strip right side down on the yellow and sew. Press the black strip upward. Sew remaining 1" sleeve strips in place: black, red, black and finish by adding the 1 1/2" sleeve strip (Fig. 3). Sew completed sleeve strips to uniform completing Unit 2.

4. Sew Unit 1 to Unit 2. Press seam toward Unit 1. Add long background strips to sides. Press toward background.
5. Cut stencil and position on face so circles are about 1/2" from mustache seam. Squirt Dizzle Dizzle on your finger and rub over the stencil to "paint." Let dry overnight.

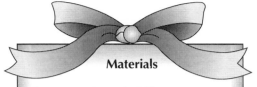

Materials

For approximately 36" square
1/2 yard red solid
1/2 yard black
1/4 yard flesh
1/4 yard or fat quarter stripe (Drosselmeyer's shirt)
1/4 yard or fat quarter stripe (Clara's bodice)
1/8 yard yellow or gold print
1/4 yard or fat quarter white stripe (beard)
1/4 yard or fat quarter gray print
1 1/4 yard red paisley print (background, border, binding)
1/2 yard green solid (sashing)
1 yard backing
Scraps of flat lace, about 1" wide
About 15" of ruffled lace, 1 1/2" wide
Scrap of fusible adhesive
4 small shirt buttons
Charm (Clara's necklace)
Crystal or pink Dizzle Dizzle paint
Black embroidery floss or Pigma 01 marker

Templates on page 58

Nutcracker Block: Cut
(1) 6 1/2" x 2 1/2" black (hat)
(2) 2 1/2" x 1" black (epaulets)
(4) 2 1/2" x 1" black (sleeve stripes)
(1) 6 1/2" x 1 1/2" yellow (brim)
(2) 2 1/2" x 1" yellow (fringe)
(1) 6 1/2" x 3 1/2" flesh (face)
(2) 2 1/2" x 3 1/2" red (sleeves)
(2) 2 1/2" x 1" red (sleeves)
(2) 2 1/2" x 1 1/2" red (sleeves)
(2) A, red (jacket)
(1) 6 1/2" x 1 1/2" white stripe (mustache)
(1) B, white stripe
(2) 6 1/2" x 2 1/2" background
(2) 12 1/2" x 1 1/2" background

Fig. 1

Fig. 2

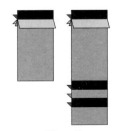

Fig. 3

Clara Block: Cut
(1) 6 1/2" x 2 1/2" yellow (bangs)
(2) C, yellow (hair)
(1) 6 1/2" x 6 1/2" flesh (face)
(1) B, stripe (bodice)
(2) A, red (dress)
(2) 6 1/2" x 2 1/2" red (sleeves)
(2) C, background
(2) 12 1/2" x 1 1/2" background

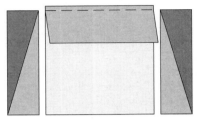

Fig. 4

Drosselmeyer Block: Cut
(1) 6 1/2" x 2 1/2" gray (hair)
(1) 6 1/2" x 4 1/2" flesh (face)
(2) A, red (vest)
(2) 6 1/2" x 2 1/2" stripe (shirt sleeves)
(1) B, stripe (bodice)
(1) D, black (eye patch)
(2) 6 1/2" x 2 1/2" background
(2) 12 1/2" x 1 1/2" background

Fig. 5

6. Draw or embroider eyes and nose.

Clara Block
Requires 3 templates: A, B and C

1. Lay pieces in order before sewing.
2. Unit 1: Head. Lay the bangs strip right side up on top of the face square. Baste across top.
3. Sew yellow C to background C to form a rectangle. Make 2. Press toward background. Sew to either side of the face. Press away from face. (Fig. 4)
4. Unit 2: Dress. Sew A's to either side of B. Press toward A. Sew a piece of lace to each sleeve so it finishes about 1" from the bottom. Sew sleeves to either side of dress body. Press seams toward dress body. Sew ruffled lace on top of the A/B seam.
5. Sew Unit 1 to Unit 2. Press toward Unit 1. Add long background strips to sides. Press toward background.
6. Stencil cheeks.
7. Draw or embroider eyes and mouth.

Drosselmeyer Block
Requires 3 templates: A, B and D

1. Lay all pieces in order before sewing.
2. Unit 1: Head. Cut a piece of fusible adhesive to match the eye patch, D, for a facing. Stitch together on the two short sides of the triangle. Trim corner and turn right side out. Make the corner as pointy as possible, being careful that the facing doesn't come apart. Finger press the seam flat. Position on the face, black side up, about 1/4" from the left edge, raw edges even with the top. Press so eye patch adheres to the face. (Fig. 5)
Sew hair strip to face. Press toward hair. Add short background strips and press toward background.
3. Unit 2: Shirt and Vest. Sew A's to either side of B. Press toward A. Sew a piece of lace to each sleeve so it finishes about 1" from the top. Sew to either side of shirt/vest. Press seams toward vest.
4. Sew Unit 1 to Unit 2. Press toward Unit 1. Add long background strips to sides and press toward background.
5. Sew shirt buttons in place.
6. Stencil cheeks.
7. Draw or embroider eye and mouth.

The Mouse King Block

Requires 4 templates: A, B, E and F

1. Lay all pieces in order before sewing.

2. Unit 1: Head. Sew spikes of crown. Press seams in one direction (Fig. 6)

Sew to 6 1/2" x 2 1/2" yellow strip to complete crown. Press toward strip. Sew to gray upper face strip. Press toward gray. Sew short background strips to either side. Press toward background.

3. Unit 2: Lower Face/Jacket. Lay the 1 1/2" x 2" black strip right side down on B, 1 1/4" from the bottom. Stitch across. (Fig. 7)

Press down. Turn the piece over and trim the black to match the edges of B.

Pin nose on either side and sew A's to either side of B. Press toward A. Sew both sleeves the same as for the Nutcracker.

4. Sew Unit 1 to Unit 2. Press seam toward Unit 1. Add long background strips to sides. Press toward background.

5. Draw or embroider eyes.

Sew the top:

1. Cut 12 green sashing strips, 12 1/2" x 2 1/2". From background, cut 9 setting squares, 2 1/2".

2. Sew 3 rows of sashing: square, strip, square, strip, square. Press seams toward squares.

3. Position blocks and sew rows: strip, block, strip, block, strip. Press seams toward blocks.

4. Sew a sashing row between the rows of blocks. Sew the other sashing rows to top and bottom. Press seams toward blocks.

5. Sew a 1" black border strip to each side and trim the excess. Sew black strips to the top and bottom and trim. Press toward black.

6. Sew a 2 1/2" paisley strip to each side and trim. Sew paisley strips to the top and bottom and trim. Press toward paisley.

7. Layer the backing, batting and quilt top and baste every 2". Quilt as desired.

8. Trim edges even with quilt top. Measure the width of the quilt and add seam allowance to either side. Cut the 3 1/2" paisley strip this width and hem the sides. Pin it across the top edge of the quilt, right side up, raw edges even.

9. Bind the edges, catching the top of the hanging sleeve in the binding. Blindstitch the bottom edge of the sleeve in place.

10. Cut the fringe strips on the blocks every 1/4".

The Mouse King Block: Cut
(1) 6 1/2" x 2 1/2" yellow (crown)
(2) E, yellow (middle crown spikes)
(2) F, yellow (outside crown spikes)
(3) E, background
(2) 6 1/2" x 2 1/2" background
(2) A, red (jacket)
(2) 2 1/2" x 3 1/2" red (sleeve)
(2) 2 1/2" x 1" red (sleeve)
(2) 2 1/2" x 1 1/2" red (sleeve)
(2) 2 1/2" x 1" black (epaulets)
(4) 2 1/2" x 1" black (sleeve stripes)
(1) 1 1/2" x 2" black (nose)
(2) 2 1/2" x 1" yellow (fringe)
(1) 6 1/2" x 3 1/2" gray (face)
(1) B, gray (lower face)

Fig. 6

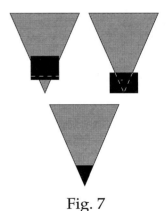

Fig. 7

Assembly: Cut
(4) 1" x 44", black (inner border)
(8) 2 1/2" x 44" red paisley print (4 for outer border, 4 for binding)
(1) 3 1/2" x 44" red paisley print (hanging sleeve)

49

Photo Album

Personalize your album by writing any message you like on the appliquéd banner and display a family photo in the oval. You don't have to be an expert at machine quilting to make a small piece like this. I used red thread on the top and in the bobbin, in case it showed through, but you can use monofilament thread if you like. (Refer to the Techniques section.) If you'd rather hand quilt, appliqué the ribbon banner first and then quilt. You could also appliqué the holly leaves before quilting, instead of making them three-dimensional.

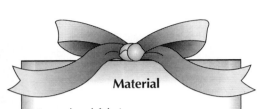

Material

1 yard red fabric
1/2 yard muslin
Fat quarter or 1/8 yard of gold fabric
Approximately 18" x 24" piece of fleece
Scraps of light, medium and dark green fabrics
Fusible adhesive
2' length of 1/4" satin ribbon or cord
1 package red piping
4 large brass grommets and setting tools
1 package of 4mm red glass beads
1 package of iridescent seed beads
Standard-size scrapbook pages (available in card shops)
Family photo that will fit behind the oval
Clear template plastic, same size as the photo
4 pieces of 2-ply chipboard: (2) 10" x 13" and (2) 1 1/8" x 13" available in art supply stores
Small awl
Xacto™ Knife

Templates on page 57

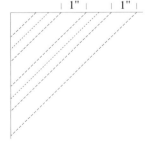

Fig. 1

Machine quilt front and back.

1. Cut 2 pieces each of red fabric, muslin and fleece, about 13" x 15".

2. For a "plaid" quilting design, mark diagonal lines on the muslin, corner to corner, that are 1" apart.

3. Go back and draw a line between two lines. Leave a 1" space and draw a line between the next two lines. Repeat. (Fig. 1) Draw diagonal lines in the other direction (in similar fashion), beginning corner to corner. Mark both pieces of muslin.

4. Lay a piece of red wrong side up, then lay the fleece and the marked muslin on top. Pin intermittently, between the marked lines. Check the front to be sure it was pinned smoothly. Repeat with the other pieces.

5. Stitch on the pencil lines. Be easy on the "gas pedal" and keep the needle down in the fabric when you stop to relocate your hands.

6. Trim each piece to 12 3/4" x 13".

7. On the right sides, pin the end of the piping in the middle of the left edge, leaving a tail about 2" long off the edge. With raw edges even, sew piping in place, clipping at each corner to make the turn. Overlap and end off with another tail coming off the edge. (Fig. 2)

The oval

1. On the wrong side, draw a vertical line 2 1/2" from the left edge. Draw a horizontal line 3 3/4" from the bottom edge. Align the oval pattern and trace. (Fig. 3)

2. Cut the oval out, 1/4" inside the traced line. (Fig. 4)

3. Fold the fabric to mark the bottom center of the oval. On the right side, pin the end of the piping at the center, coming off the edge as you did before. Sew in place, overlapping the ends. (Fig. 5)

4. Face the opening. Cut a 6 1/2" x 5" piece of muslin and pin it to the front, over the hole. Stitch from the back, directly on top of the piping seam, all the way around the opening. Cut away the center and clip the seam allowance. Turn the facing to the wrong side through the hole and pin. Machine stitch all around, 1" away from the piped edge.

5. Sew a "pocket" to hold the photo in place. (Don't tape the photo behind the opening; the tape will dry out over time.)

Cut 1" wide strips of fabric the same length as the sides of the photo, plus 1/2". Fold the strips lengthwise and press. Cut into 4 equal pieces.

6. From the right side, position the photo behind the oval. When you have it where you like it, turn everything over and trace the photo onto the muslin.

7. With a running stitch or backstitch through the muslin only, sew the strips across each corner, using the pencil line as a guide. (Fig. 6)

8. Cover the photo with clear plastic and pop them into the "corners." (Fig. 7) Trim just a bit if they don't quite fit. Take them back out and hold them for later.

Ribbon banner

1. For patterns, trace the three banner pieces on page 57. Cut out, adding about 1/8" seam allowance. Lay them wrong side up on the ironing board and press a piece of freezer paper to them. Write the title with a smooth hand (see Techniques), add lots of close dots for shadows if you like, and remove the paper.

2. Baste the raw edges of the three pieces to prepare each one for stitching. (This isn't necessary if you didn't machine quilt.) Do not baste areas that will be covered by another piece. Baste curves carefully.

3. Lay the pieces in place, referring to the cover photo. The top piece should be about 1 1/2" from the top edge and 1 3/4" from the right edge; the bottom piece shouldn't come down any farther than 5" from the top edge.

4. Appliqué the banner.

Lining

1. Lay the front and back pieces on red fabric and cut lining to size.

2. Pin right sides together and stitch on the seam made by the piping, leaving the left side of the front unstitched.

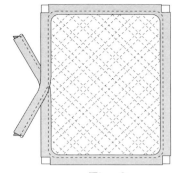

Fig. 2

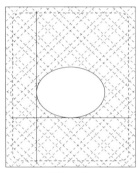

Fig. 3

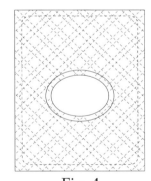

Fig. 4

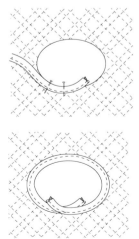

Fig. 5

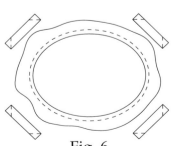

Fig. 6

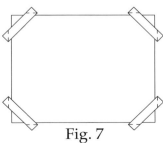

Fig. 7

51

Repeat for the back, leaving the right side unstitched. Clip corners and turn right side out.

Holly leaves

1. Fuse green fabrics together (one fabric can be used for all the back sides). Cut out a variety of leaves; I cut mine freehand, out of 1" squares of fused fabric.

2. Using the stitchline as a guide, arrange leaves around the opening. Tack in place with green thread.

3. Sew red beads in groups of three here and there.

Finishing

1. Place photo and plastic covering behind the oval and insert one large piece of board through the side opening. Change to the zipper foot and machine stitch against the board to enclose it.

2. Lay the small boards on a sheet of scrapbook paper and mark the holes (about 3 1/2" on either side of the center). Use an awl to poke the holes in the board; trim the holes with an Xacto™ knife until the grommets fit.

3. Insert one of these boards in the remaining opening on the front and blindstitch closed, behind the piping. This is the spine of the book.

4. Sew the back of the album the same way.

5. Line up the awl with the pre-made holes and poke through the fabric. Set the grommets in place.

6. Thread ribbon or cording through the front, the pages and the back, then across the back and up to the front. Tie a square knot and then a bow.

Wonder-of-a-Kind Christmas Cards

Fused fabrics make quick, one of a kind fabric cards for unique individuals.

Beary Christmas

This is a drawing of a bear that lives in my office.

1. Apply Wonder Under® to a 6 1/2" square of a light check or other light fabric with a directional print. Fuse a scrap of Wonder Under® to a small piece of red fabric for the bow.

2. Trace the pattern onto typing paper, using a marker so the lines will be very dark.

3. On a lightbox, trace the pattern on the right side of the fused fabric. Turn the fabric each time you trace a new piece, so the check will be slightly askew when the pieces touch each other. Cut out the pieces and peel off the papers.

4. Place a light colored 6 1/2" background square over the pattern on the lightbox. Using a brown Pigma 01 marker, write your greeting. Arrange the head pieces on the square and carefully carry it to the ironing board. Press the pieces in place. Repeat with two or three pieces until finished.

5. Lay the block face down on a backing square and place this on a piece of batting. Sew all around, leaving a 4" opening at the bottom for turning(Fig. 1).

6. Clip corners and turn. Blindstitch opening closed. Quilt if desired.

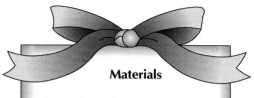

Materials

(for each card)
Pellon® Wonder Under®
1" strips for border
6 1/2" square of backing fabric
Country hanger with 2 tiny clothespins
Very sharp, small scissors
(2) 6 1/2" squares of fabric; read specific instructions for color suggestions

Templates on page 54 & 59

Fig. 1

From Our House to Yours

I cut small motifs of a tree and a wreath from a printed fabric and fused them behind the window and on the door.

1. Apply Wonder Under® to a 3" x 4 1/2" piece of white fabric.

2. Trace the pattern onto typing paper, using a marker so the lines will be very dark.

3. On the lightbox, trace the pattern on the paper side of the fused fabric. Cut out the pieces and peel off the papers.

4. Cut a 3" x 4 1/2" piece of "snowy sky" fabric. Position the white cutout on the sky fabric. Tuck the tree behind the window and add a wreath to the door, if desired. Press all pieces to fuse.

5. Cut a 2" x 4 1/2" piece of white and stitch it to the bottom of the fused unit. Press seam allowance toward this piece.

6. Sew 3/4" strips on all 4 sides, trimming excess each time.

7. Lay the block face down on a backing square and place this on a piece of batting. Sew all around, leaving a 4" opening at the bottom for turning.

8. Clip corners and turn. Blindstitch opening closed. Quilt or draw stitches with a Pigma 01 marker.

9. Inscribe the block with your sentiment.

Snowflake

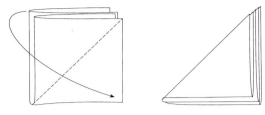

Fig. 2

Remember cutting paper snowflakes? This time, use fused fabric!

1. Apply Wonder Under® to a 6 1/2" square of white fabric that has been spray starched. Fold the fused fabric in half, finger-pressing a hard crease. Fold again (into fourths), crease and fold again (into eighths) (Fig. 2).

2. Cut a different design on each side. Hold the fabric tightly between your fingers, maneuvering it and the scissors as needed. Don't worry if you can't make a perfect cut; it can be cleaned up later (Fig. 3).

3. Open the snowflake and snip off any fabric that wasn't completely cut away. Your snowflake may need some detailing, like mine. Just fold each stem down the center and snip here and there. Snip opposite stems so they look more or less symmetrical. (Unlike the real things, fabric snowflakes are not perfect! But if you don't like the one you cut, throw it away and cut another one. Try folding the fabric into fourths instead of eighths.) (Fig. 4)

4. Peel the paper off and lay the snowflake on a 6 1/2" red square. Smooth all the stems and press to fuse it to the background. *Optional: Add additional cut motifs to fill in around the snowflake.*

5. Using a black Pigma 01 marker, draw very small "quilting stitches" to outline the snowflake.

6. Right sides together, sew a 1" strip to one side and trim off the excess strip. Rotate the block a quarter-turn and sew another border. Repeat for all 4 sides.

7. Using a brown or black Pigma 01 marker, write your sentiment on a 6 1/2" square of light colored backing fabric.

8. Place the block on the signed square, right sides together. Pin to a 6 1/2" square of batting and sew all around, leaving a 4" opening at the bottom for turning.

9. Clip corners and turn. Blindstitch opening closed.

Fig. 3

From Our House to Yours

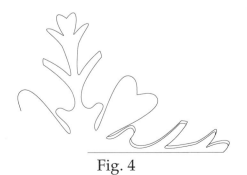

Fig. 4

Gift Box

For special gifts or special friends! This 8" box is as much a gift as what's inside it, and the recipient will enjoy using it year-round. Pop a handwritten note inside, suggesting a variety of uses, such as holding hair ribbons, keepsakes or spools of thread. Let the kids make one-of-a-kind cloth for Gramma's gift box. Turn them loose with muslin and fabric markers. When the box is finished, have them sign the bottom with their names and ages.

Make (4) 8" Christmas Tree blocks

1. Row 1: Sew A and AR to either side of B triangle. (Fig. 1)

2. Row 2: Sew C and CR to either side of D.

3. Row 3: Sew E and ER to either side of F.

4. Row 4: Sew G and GR to either side of H.

5. Press all rows at one time, pressing seams toward background.

6. Sew Rows together and press seams upward on 2 blocks and downward on 2 blocks. (Sew blocks alternately when making box, so seams will butt nicely.)

7. Square up all 4 blocks and trim top and bottom pieces to the same size.

Make the box

1. Sew the blocks together in this arrangement: (Fig. 2) Press.

2. Lay this piece on the lining fabric, right sides together, and pin. Sew all around, pivoting at corners and leaving the bottom edge open. (Fig. 3)

3. Trim corners and clip into angles. Turn right side out. Push the corners out sharply and press.

4. Work with the patchwork side up. Measure each block and get an average size.

5. Mark 6 squares this size on the board. Place the cutting

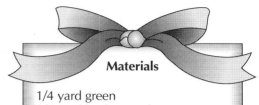

Materials

1/4 yard green
1/4 yard background
1 yard lining
(2) 9" squares for top and bottom
(4) 18" lengths of 1" ribbon
1 sheet of 3/16" chipboard
(available in art supply stores)

Templates on page 59

Cutting
Cut 4 each A, C, E, G, background
Cut 4 each B, D, F, H, green
Cut 4 each AR, CR, ER, GR, background
Cut (1) 8 1/2" square, background for top
Cut (2) 8 1/2" squares, green for bottom

Fig. 1

Block or decorative fabric	Top of box		
		Sides of box	
Block or decorative fabric	Block or decorative fabric	Block or decorative fabric	Block or decorative fabric
	Lining or decorative fabric		
	Bottom of box		

Fig. 2

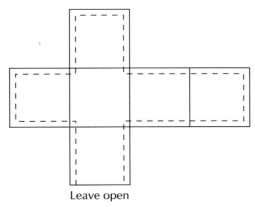

Leave open

Fig. 3

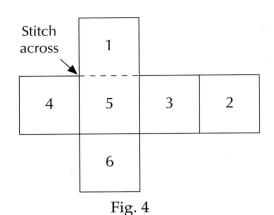

Stitch across

	1		
4	5	3	2
	6		

Fig. 4

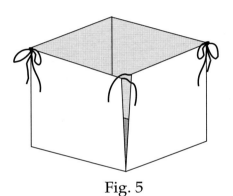

Fig. 5

mat under the board and rotary-cut on the pencil line three or four times before moving the ruler. Bend the board forward to snap it apart.

6. Fit each board into the lining individually. Place the board on top of the block first to see how it will fit; trim, if necessary. (I almost always have to trim my boards. Even though I trim the blocks square so they are all the same size, and cut the boards exactly, sometimes my seams aren't all the same 1/4".) If a board is just a bit on the small side, that's okay. The box will still work out. Insert the first board in the top, adjusting the seam allowance so it's on the lining side of the board, and stitch across.

7. Insert other boards, one at a time, in the order shown. For small boxes, stitch in the ditch between blocks as each board is inserted. (Fig. 4)

8. Insert the last board and blindstitch the opening closed.

9. Fold into a box shape. If the lining is loose, take a few stitches by hand between the boards so the inside corners will be sharp.

10. Blindstitch the sides and bottom together (a regular needle is just as easy to use as a curved needle). Or stitch ribbon ties to each corner and tie the sides together. (Fig. 5)

11. For package ties, fold the raw edge under and sew a length of ribbon to the center of each side. (Fig. 6)

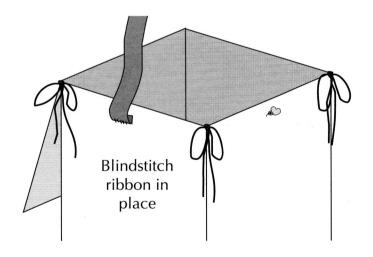

Blindstitch ribbon in place

Fig. 6

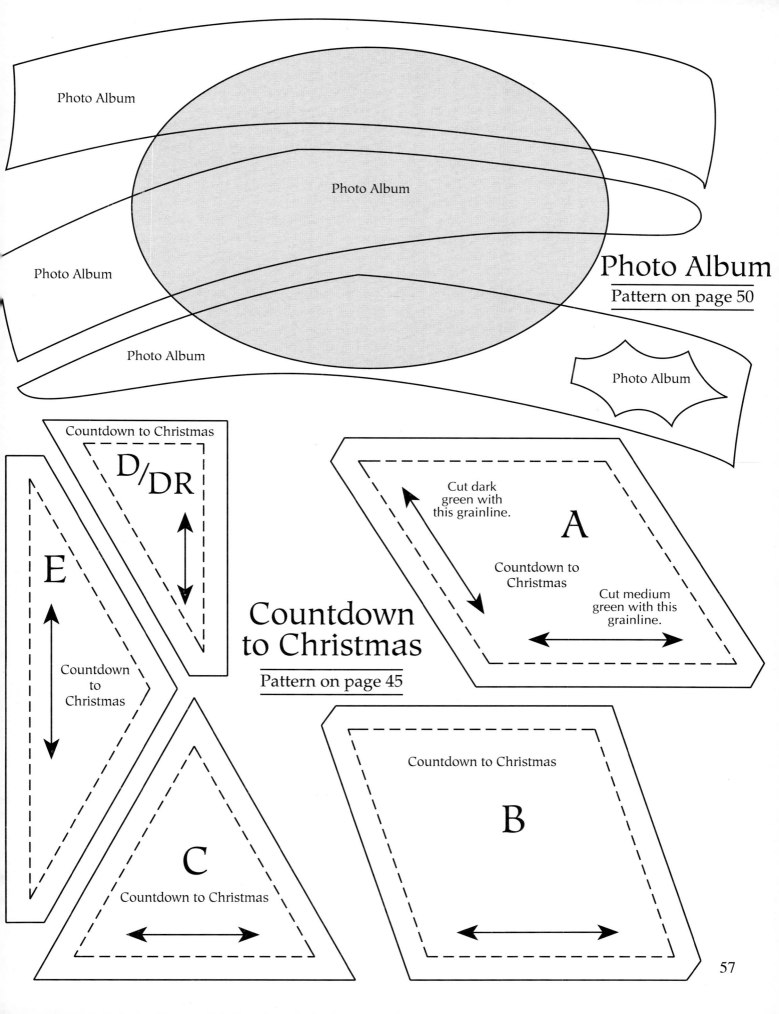

Photo Album

Photo Album

Photo Album

Photo Album

Photo Album

Photo Album
Pattern on page 50

Photo Album

Countdown to Christmas

D/DR

E

Countdown to Christmas

Countdown to Christmas
Pattern on page 45

Cut dark green with this grainline.

A

Countdown to Christmas

Cut medium green with this grainline.

Countdown to Christmas

B

C

Countdown to Christmas

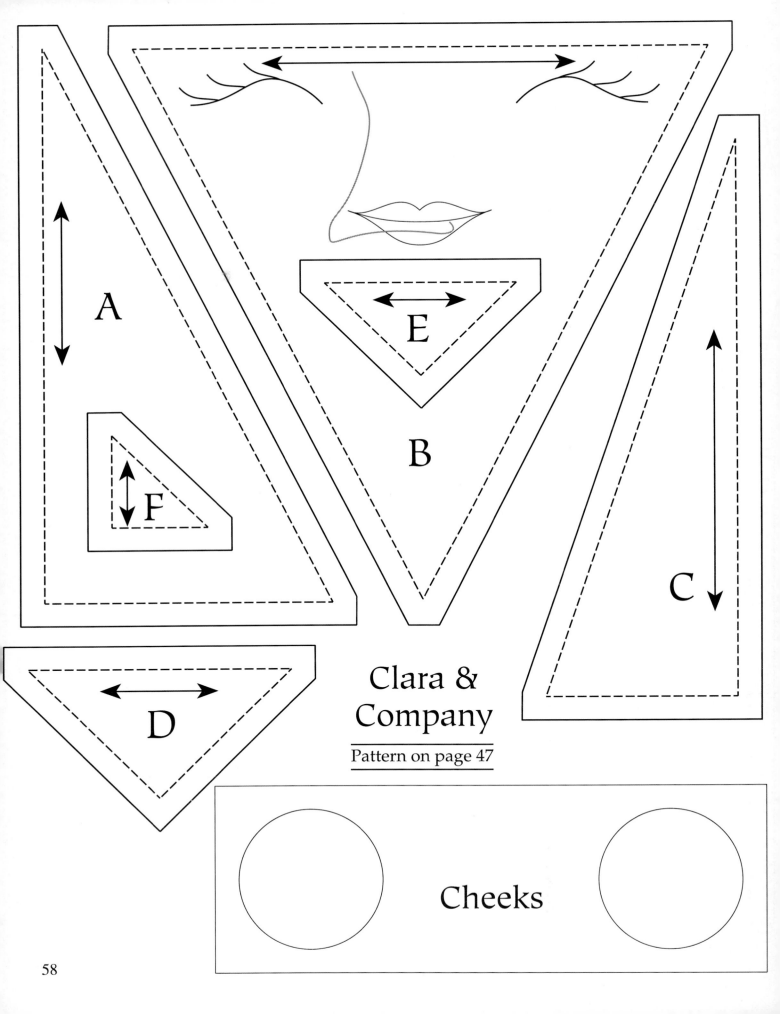

A

E

B

F

C

D

Clara &
Company

Pattern on page 47

Cheeks

58

Beary Christmas

Pattern on page 53

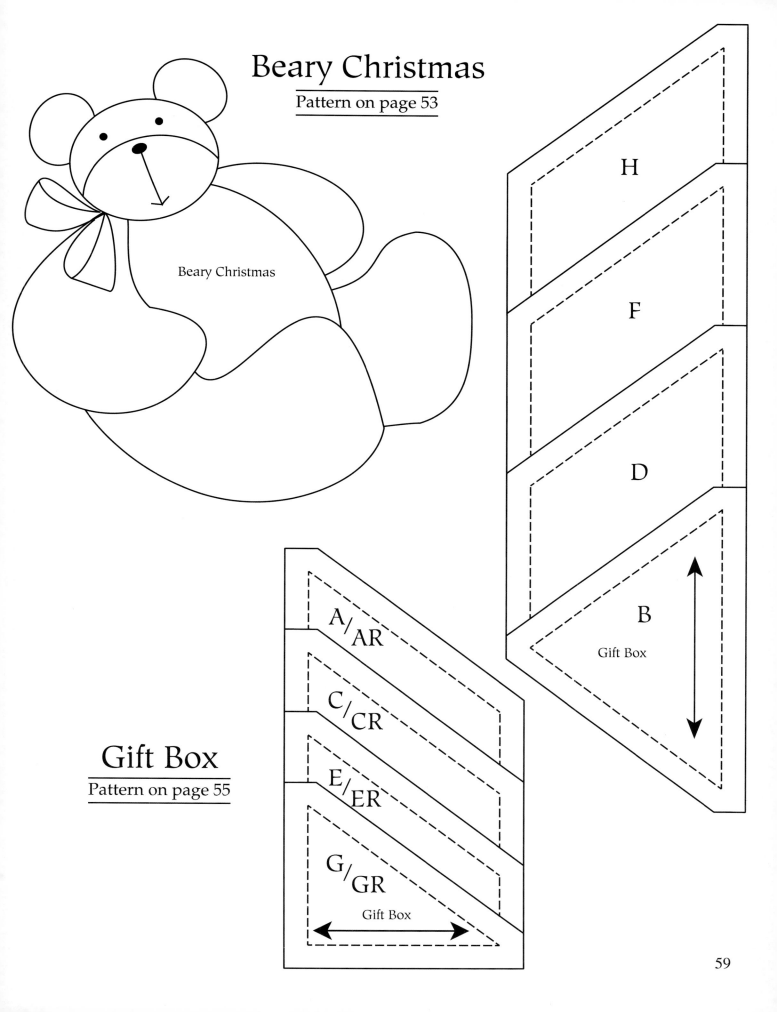

Beary Christmas

H

F

D

B

Gift Box

Gift Box

Pattern on page 55

A/AR

C/CR

E/ER

G/GR

Gift Box

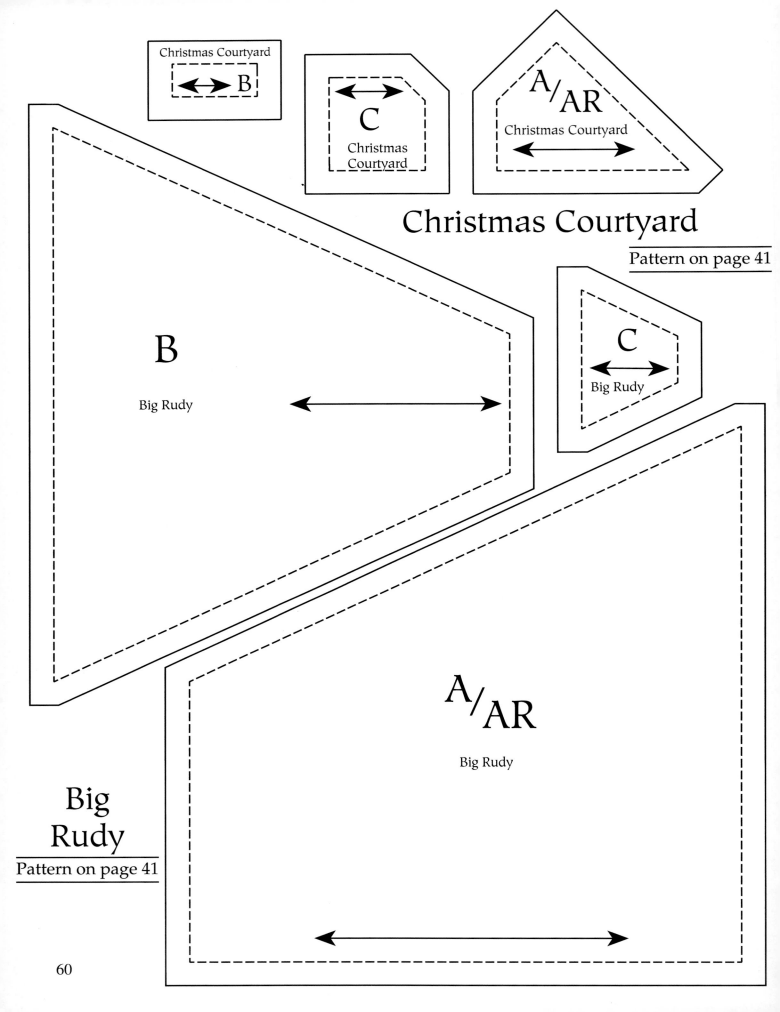

Christmas Courtyard

← → B

C

Christmas
Courtyard

A/AR

Christmas Courtyard

Christmas Courtyard

Pattern on page 41

C

Big Rudy

B

Big Rudy

A/AR

Big Rudy

Big Rudy

Pattern on page 41

Merry Kitty

Pattern on page 21

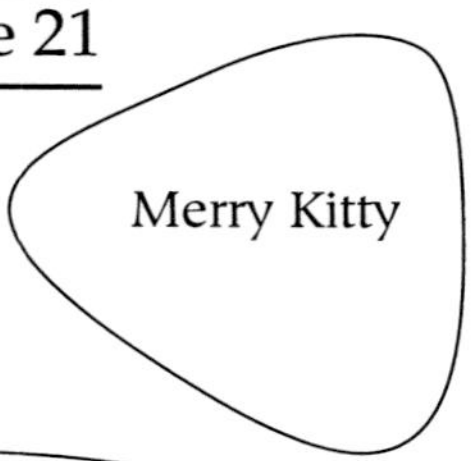

Add 1/4" seam
allowance

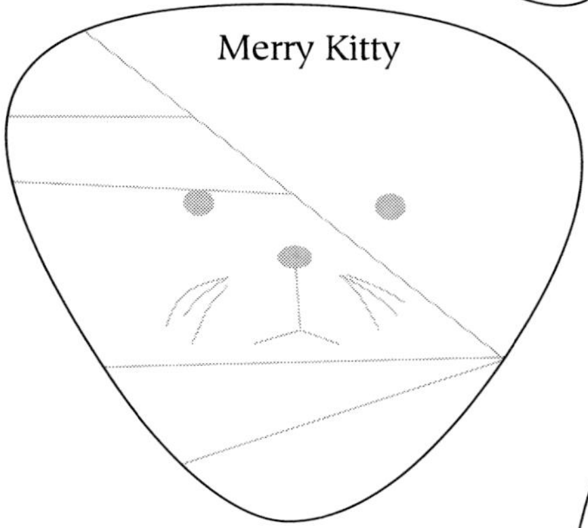

Merry Kitty

Merry Kitty

Friendship's Offering

Pattern on page 18

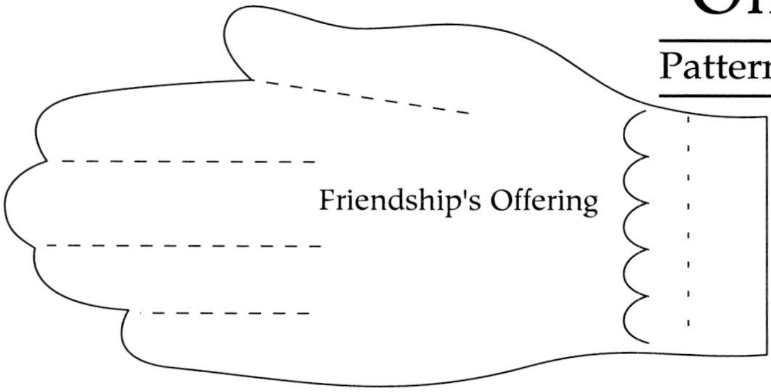

Friendship's Offering

Add 1/4"
seam
allowance

Baby's First Christmas

Pattern on page 18

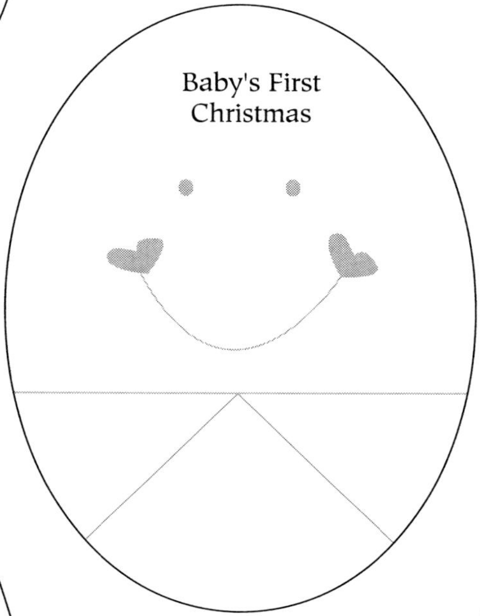

Baby's First
Christmas

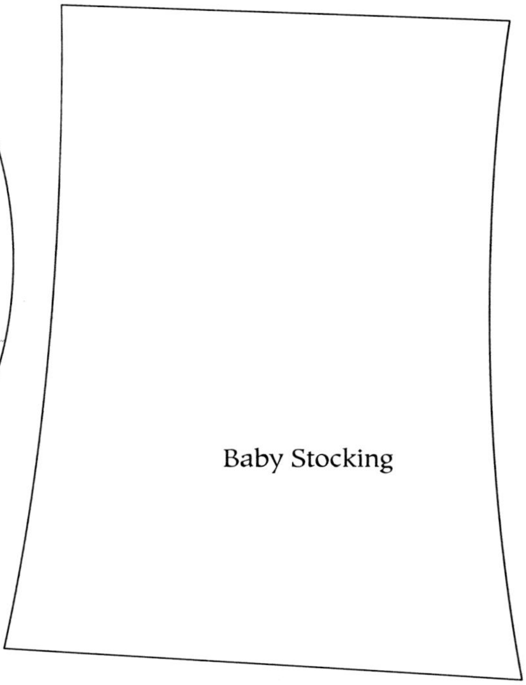

Baby Stocking

Folk Stars

Pattern on page 21

Folk Stars

Baby Stocking

Pattern on page 20

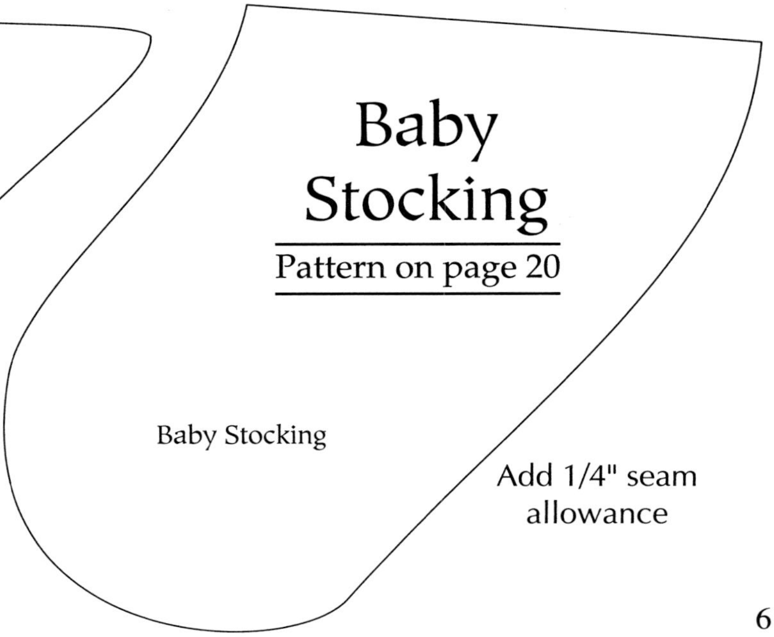

Baby Stocking

Add 1/4" seam
allowance

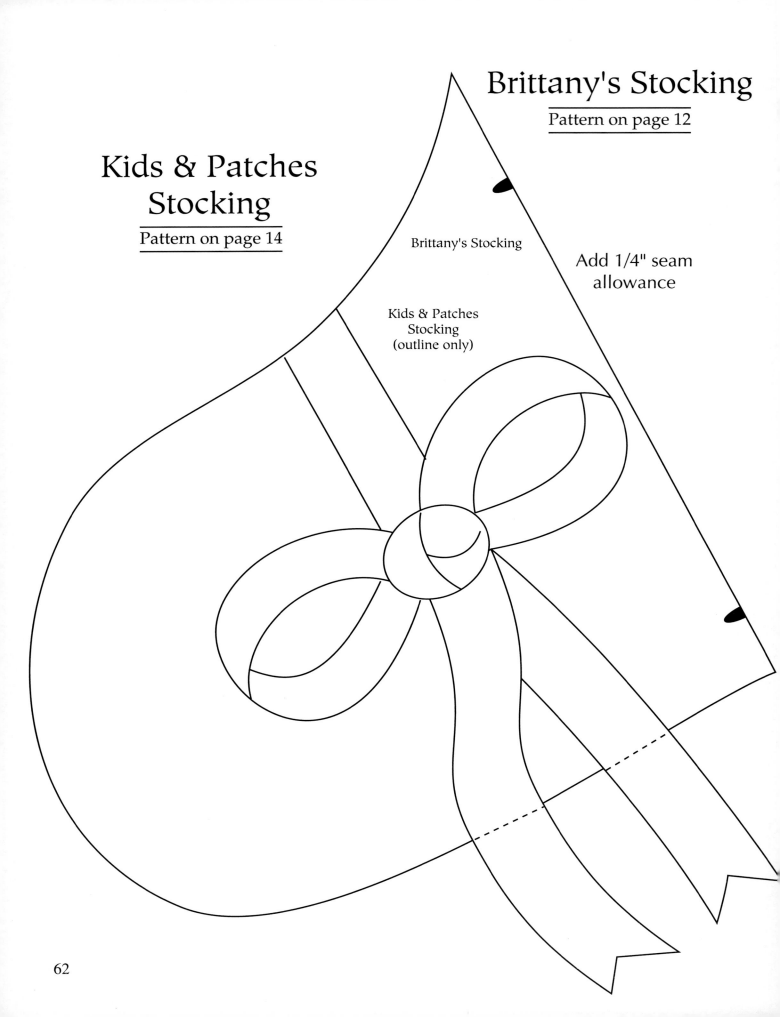

Brittany's Stocking

Pattern on page 12

Kids & Patches Stocking

Pattern on page 14

Brittany's Stocking

Kids & Patches
Stocking
(outline only)

Add 1/4" seam
allowance

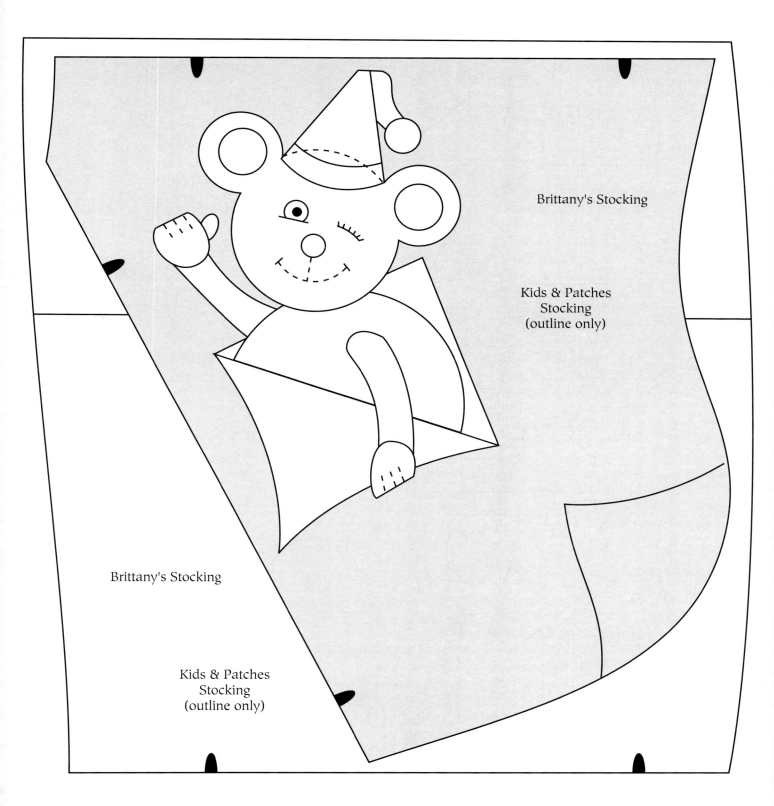

Brittany's Stocking

Kids & Patches
Stocking
(outline only)

Brittany's Stocking

Kids & Patches
Stocking
(outline only)

Add 1/4" seam allowance

Roly Poly Santa

Add 1/4"
seam
allowance

Roly Poly Santa

slit here

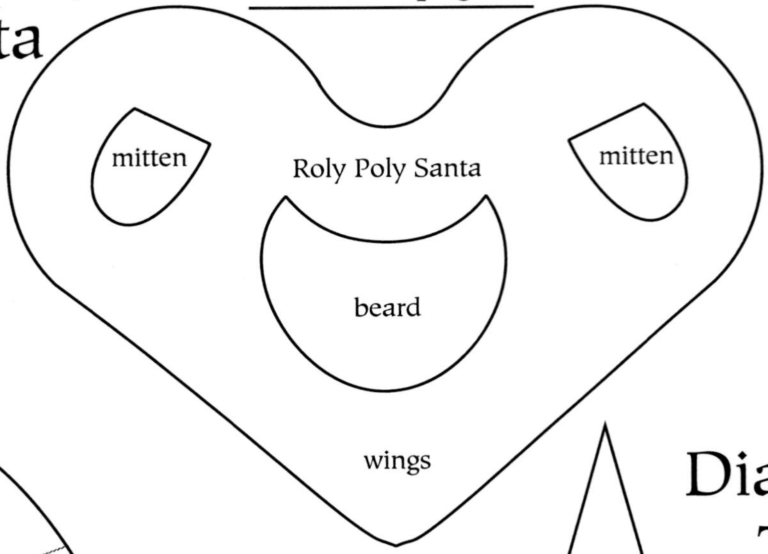

Pattern on page 19

mitten

Roly Poly Santa

mitten

beard

wings

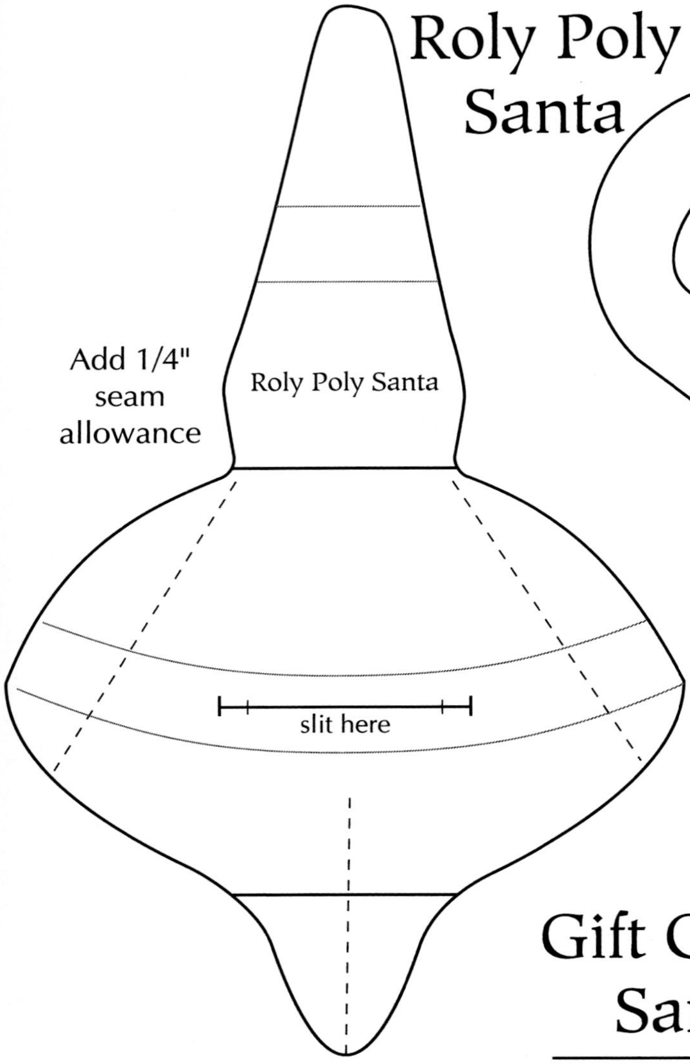

Diamond Tree

Pattern on page 44

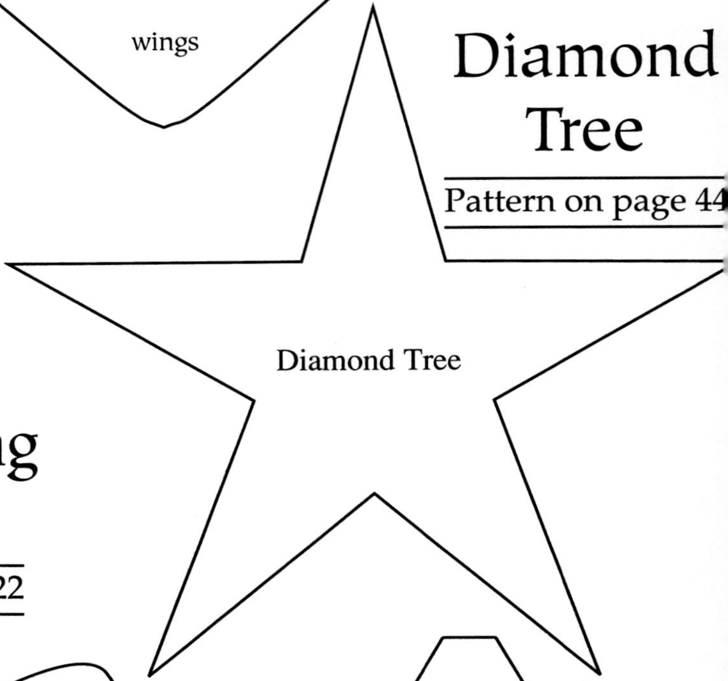

Diamond Tree

Gift Giving Santa

Pattern on page 22

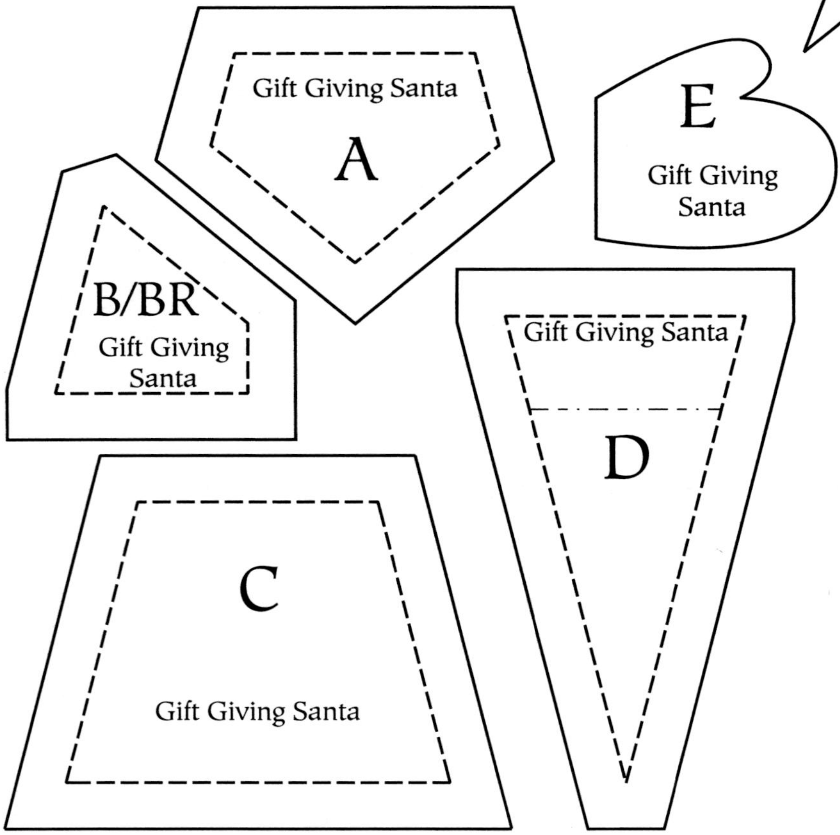

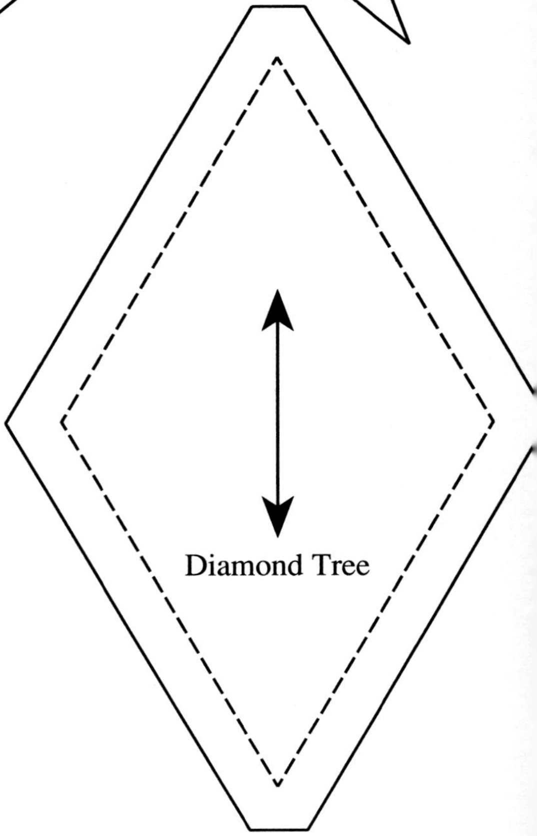

Gift Giving Santa

A

B/BR
Gift Giving Santa

C

Gift Giving Santa

E
Gift Giving Santa

Gift Giving Santa

D

Diamond Tree

Santa Dolls, Big and Small

Pattern on page 28

Trace twice and tape together for complete pattern.

Add 1/4" seam allowances

Bibliography

Books on quiltmaking techniques
Appliqué 12 Easy Ways © 1991 by Elly Sienkiewicz. C & T Publishing, Martinez, CA
Quilts! Quilts! Quilts! © 1988 by Diane McClun. Quilt Digest Press, San Francisco, CA
From Basics to Binding: *A Complete Guide to Making Quilts* © 1992 by Karen Kay Buckley. AQS, Paducah, KY

Books on rotary cutting
Timeless Treasures, The Complete Book on Rotary Cutting © 1992 by Nancy Johnson-Srebro.
RCW Publishing Company, Columbia Crossroads, PA
Tiny Traditions, © 1992 by Sylvia Voudrie. Chitra Publications, Montrose, PA

Magazines about quiltmaking. Patti Bachelder, Editor
Quilting Today, Traditional Quiltworks and *Miniature Quilts*. Chitra Publications, Montrose, PA

A book of Christmas sentiments
Christmas Tidings. Edited by Louise Bachelder, © 1984 by Peter Pauper Press, Inc., White Plains, NY

Resources

Portable tracing table: Give Me Light!
Me Sew, Inc.
24307 Magic Mountain Parkway, Suite 195
Valencia, CA 91355
(800) 846-3739

Handmade bent wire hangers with mini clothespins
The Quilt Patch
221 Old Stage Way
Yakima, WA 98908

Pigma Pens, books on writing and friendship sentiments
Wallflower Designs
1573 Millersville Rd.
Millersville, MD 21108

Rotary cutting supplies, books and other quilting supplies
The Quilters Treasure Box
2 Public Avenue
Montrose, PA 18801
(800) 278-2227

Dizzle Dizzle paint, quilting and dollmaking supplies
Osage County Quilt Factory
400 Walnut, Box 490
Overbrook, KS 66524

Sewing machine feet for 1/4" seams and machine quilting
Little Foot, Ltd.
605 Bledsoe, NW
Albuquerque, NM 87107